Praise for
A Bump in Life

There is nothing as truly wonderful as finding out you're pregnant unless the timing feels off. Of all the options available to pregnant women facing hardships, the choice to give birth requires the most courage. At Gateway Church, we put a big emphasis on helping single-parent families, and we are so proud of what Amy Ford has done with Embrace Grace.

In *A Bump in Life*, Amy shares her insights along with the courageous stories of women who chose life when they discovered they were pregnant. Their stories will inspire and encourage you.

Robert and Debbie Morris,
Founding Senior Pastor and
Executive Pastor of Gateway Church

Great lessons are learned when we go from a breakdown into a breakthrough. *A Bump in Life* gives incredible pictures of precious lives that were on the verge of a breakdown and shows how they kept walking toward their redemptive breakthrough. The stories are real. Each page holds within it such truth that God will never leave us no matter what our situation. As you read each story, you can see, not only did Amy's ministry help these girls to *know*

Jesus, but they helped them *walk* with Him. Their testimonies ring true with clarity and should give every reader renewed hope that even though we may have bumps in life, God turns every situation that seems hopeless into a beautiful blessing!

Kerrie Oles, Living Divine Ministries,
author of *Invisible Chains,* and Freedom teacher
at Gateway Church

As I read the heart-wrenching stories of *A Bump in Life* of these young women who are faced with an unplanned pregnancy, my heart is even more stirred to tell the world abortion in not an option. I applaud Amy Ford and the work she is doing with Embrace Grace. This book will be a tool to penetrate the darkness and light the pathway for young women to experience God's beautiful peace and restoration.

Joni Lamb, host of *The Joni Show,*
Daystar Television Network

My mom was encouraged to abort her first baby due to major health concerns; she chose life. I am glad she did because I wouldn't have been able to be born and live out the calling God has on my life. Wherever you find your story, hold onto Jesus and trust that He'll walk you through this season because the little life inside of you wants to impact this world for Jesus. *A Bump in Life* will give you hope to walk this out!

Kari Jobe
worship leader, artist, and songwriter

I picked up *A Bump in Life* intending to just start a chapter, but as I read I couldn't put it down. As a woman who found herself pregnant and unmarried, I wish I had chosen life as these brave women in the stories have. Story after story stirred my heart and reminded me of God's goodness. Amy Ford unveils lives that inspire each of us to embrace grace, even in the hardest of circumstances.

Irini Fambro, Ordained Pastor and Master of Divinity
from Beeson Divinity School and
author of *Made for More*

For many of us, some of the greatest blessings of our lives began with an "Oh no!" moment. What we thought was the end of something was in fact the birth of a new beginning. So it was for Amy Ford and the countless young women she has walked through an unplanned pregnancy.

Having had a front row seat to the birth of Embrace Grace, I can say with certainty that Amy is truly a Titus 2 woman. She offers a young and inexperienced mom her wisdom, encouragement, and love. As you read *A Bump in Life*, you sit in the shoes of many of those young women and experience the power of acceptance over judgment, hope over despair, and life over death. Amy's story, her heart to serve, and her willingness to pay the price to help another gives me hope—hope for these babies, hope for these women, and hope for the church.

Jan Greenwood, Pink (Gateway Women)
and author of *Women at War*

While the rest of the culture argues, postures, and politicizes, Amy Ford just practically and powerfully demonstrates love to hurting and confused girls. I love this, and so I love this book. Like the blind man who says, "all I know was I was once blind and now I see," Amy, in her book, gives girls a chance to say the same. I was once alone; now I have family. I was once afraid; now I am confident. I was once confused; now I know how to make it through. We need more Amy Fords in the world.

Bob Hamp, Executive Pastor, Pastoral Care
at Gateway Church, Licensed Marriage and
Family Therapist, and author of
Think Differently Live Differently

A BUMP IN LIFE

AMY FORD

A
BUMP
IN
LIFE

True Stories of Hope & Courage During
an Unplanned Pregnancy

PUBLISHING GROUP
NASHVILLE, TENNESSEE

978-1-4336-8187-5

Published by B&H Publishing Group
Nashville, Tennessee

Dewey Decimal Classification: 306.85
Subject Heading: TEENAGE PREGNANCY
\ TEENAGE MOTHERS \ UNMARRIED
MOTHERS

1 2 3 4 5 6 7 8 • 17 16 15 14 13

To all the brave and courageous who chose life and who taught us the lessons of life along the way.

Acknowledgments

To my sweet hubby, Ryan, whose unselfish love and extra hours taking care of the kids made the writing of this book possible. I'm so thankful for you!

And to our kids—Jess, Mackenzie, Landry, and Judah—for their patience and helping to work as a team so Mom can become an "arthur."

To Salina Duffy, my ladybug friend. Thank you for being the perfect partner with Embrace Grace. I couldn't imagine doing it with anyone else in the world. You inspire me and I'm so grateful for you.

And I'm so thankful for all my family and friends that tirelessly encouraged me through this process of writing and publishing and always cheered me on! You make life so much more fun and I love getting to walk it out with each of you.

Thank you to Jan Greenwood for taking the time out of your busy schedule to empower and inspire us to write what's on our hearts and for showing us how publishing works. If it were not for your time spent on research, this book might not be here. Thank you for always leading with grace and being such a great example for all of us.

Nancy Smith with Authority Press, you are the best writing coach and cheerleader ever! Thank you for helping me think differently and look at situations from other perspectives with my writing. I love working with you.

To my awesome agent, Rachel Kent, thank you for believing in me!

Thanks to Destiny in Bloom for giving a regular girl like me a platform to discover a writing gift I never knew I had.

Thank you to Gateway Church and my pastors, Robert and Debbie Morris, for teaching me how to hear God, equipping me and encouraging me to step into my calling by providing amazing resources and classes, and empowering me to walk out God's will for my life. You really are "all about the people."

To Pastor Samantha Golden, thank you for joining

hands with Embrace Grace and always helping us bless and minister to the sweet girls with crisis pregnancies.

To all the Embrace Grace leaders, I *love* getting to serve with all of you.

Love to all the Embrace Grace mommas out there, thank you for being so transparent and always being willing to share your story to help others. Each one of you truly inspires me and are forever my heroes.

And to my heavenly Father, without You there are no stories. You are the author of our lives and You make beautiful stories out of all of us. Thank You for giving me this passion for these baby mommas and an opportunity to write (Hab. 2:2). I love getting to do what I do. I love You so much.

Contents

Foreword

My heart was pounding in my chest. The delicate, thin voice on the other end of the line was my daughter's. I had watched her walk out the back door the night before with tears in her eyes. Attempts to solicit information from her as to what was going on had been met with the strained retort, "I'm going to spend the night with and talk to my mentor." It was really not out of the ordinary that she was experiencing some personal trauma that required emotional support from a family friend. Anyone who has ever had a teenage daughter understands.

Now it was early the next morning. Call it a father's intuition, call it discernment—call it whatever. I somehow sensed that this wasn't just another conversation regarding some boyfriend issue. Somehow, I knew that something was desperately wrong.

"I have to talk with you and Mom tonight," she murmured into the phone with a tired voice that I sensed hadn't slept much the night before. And in an instant I knew what she wanted to talk about.

After a long pause, I whispered, "Are you pregnant?"

Silence. It seemed to go on forever. I asked the question again, with more urgency.

After what seemed like an eternity, her frail voice responded with raw emotion, "Dad, I'm so sorry."

I fought back tears as I struggled to grasp what I was hearing. This was my only girl! I had so many hopes and dreams for her future. I had dreamed of giving her opportunities that I had not been afforded as a young man. There was college, there was me walking her down a flower-lined aisle in a white dress toward her prince charming . . . then after settling into marriage and adjusting to a career, *then* a baby would be a welcome and exciting addition not only to her life but mine as well. *Then*—not now.

How would I explain to the church? I was the pastor, for crying out loud! How would people respond? Adoption? Have the baby? Would my insurance cover this? Had the father been told? Where would she live? How involved will the young man be? Does she plan on marrying him? Would he bolt and run after being told the news? Would he be responsible and provide for his child, or would that responsibility fall squarely on the shoulders of my daughter? And of course, even more important, how would this affect the life of my precious daughter and my first grandchild?

An hour or so later, we sat at the end of her bed and cried together. This was one problem that I could not solve for her. As I held her, I knew that the pregnancy would change my life and hers forever; my sadness for her washed over me in waves. I wanted to be happy and celebrate the birth of my first grandchild, but this was not how the gift was supposed to be wrapped.

During the course of the next few months, when we should have been conversing about boyfriends and college, we were instead talking about doctor appointments, prenatal vitamins, morning sickness, and about adoption versus keeping the baby. It was a raw, emotional journey, and many times I felt overwhelmed by the mixture of feelings of sadness and joy all at the same time.

At some point during the course of her first trimester, my daughter was introduced to Amy Ford and the girls of Embrace Grace. Enter a young woman who had "been there" and somehow had not just survived, but had gone on to realize her purpose in life. And now, she willingly shares her life experience and gives her heart to young girls like my daughter. The journey, while still difficult, became bearable for us.

Amy's story provides encouragement in the waiting; escape from shame and guilt of unplanned miracles of grace; and comfort to parents who feel guilt and pain as well.

This book is filled with her story and others . . . including my daughter's. And while each story is unique, the Father's plan for each and every life connects them all.

And that plan doesn't have to be destroyed by an unplanned pregnancy. In fact, the Father even has a plan for the child who was, without a doubt, "planned" from before the foundation of the world.

Fast-forward. When I hold God's gift, my first granddaughter, I cannot imagine life without her. I still believe that God's purpose will be fulfilled in my daughter's life. I have witnessed firsthand God's power to save, forgive, and heal. And while each day still holds challenges and obstacles, God gives blessings and grace to face each day.

My prayer is that your life will be impacted by these stories in the same way I have been. My hope is that you will see the sunshine peeking through the clouds of confusion and despair. And above all, that you will remember, someday soon, tol thank God for this little bump in the road of life.

Dan Dean
Lead Pastor, Heartland Church, Carrollton, Texas
Lead Singer, Phillips, Craig, and Dean

Introduction

In 2008, I attended a women's conference at my home church, Gateway. The entire three-day event was about finding your place in God's kingdom: Where are you to serve in the kingdom, and what plans might God have for you?

During the last session of the conference, something began to stir deep inside me, and I just knew that God wanted to make a move in my life, that He had called me to something. I asked Him to show me what it might be. During worship, I closed my eyes; immediately, God gave me a vision.

The vision began like snapshots flashing: pictures of me, single, and pregnant. I saw the loneliness, shame, guilt, and sadness that I felt during that difficult season of my life. Then, the snapshots started changing to my life now—happy and fulfilled, with my God and my family. The snapshots changed again to me throwing baby showers for women. I *love* throwing parties for people, and that year, I had thrown thirteen baby showers!

The conference ended, and the very first thing I wanted to do was tell my friend Salina what God had shown me. Before we even left the building that day, we found a quiet corner and excitedly exchanged our "God stories." I told her about my vision, and she said she heard God speak something similar to her heart: "Help the mommies and the babies."

We had no idea what we were doing and how we were going to do it, but we knew God was up to something *big*.

That summer, we met with pastors to brainstorm about what God was stirring in our hearts. That fall, we started a small group for single and pregnant girls, and called it Embrace Grace. After we chose the name, we searched everywhere for the perfect curriculum, and we ended up finding a book called *Embrace Grace* by Liz Curtis Higgs that was perfect! Of course it was—the name and the book was part of God's plan!

Our first semester, we had three sweet girls and thus began one of the most fulfilling times of my life. I *loved* being with these girls every Monday night; I loved hearing their hearts and offering God's hope to them, encouraging them and being excited for them throughout the milestones of pregnancy.

The easier, or at least quicker, route for these girls might have been to have an abortion . . . but these girls chose *life*. They were brave enough to have their babies, and we wanted to honor them for making that courageous choice.

We met each week throughout the semester, and noticed that their walls they had built around them were slowly coming down, brick by brick. By opening up more and more, God came in and healed all their broken pieces, enabling them to be healthier, spiritually and emotionally, for their babies.

We ended the semester by organizing a baby shower for them. Donations flooded in, and we never had to use our own money. God took care of each of them.

We also organized a special night just for the mothers called Princess Day. We gave them a special invitation and told them to come in comfy clothes but bring a nice dress for a special day. We hosted Princess Day in a large home and as the girls arrived we told them that a team of hairdressers, makeup artists, and massage therapists were there to pamper them and help them to feel as beautiful on the outside as they were on the inside. The girls were in heaven, huge smiles on their faces.

As they were getting ready, the leaders and volunteers were preparing a beautifully set table with fine china and unique place settings. When they were finished getting ready, we crowned each one of them and told them how much God loves them. We wanted them to look in the mirror and see the picture of how God sees them—His princesses. His treasures. We spoke life into each one, calling out some of their gifts. After we were finished, they sat down at the table and we served them a four-course meal, including filet mignon.

By the end of the night, they had just a small taste of how much God truly loved them. They looked so beautiful with their crowns and baby bumps. Maybe if the girls could really capture and understand their value and worth, and how much God REALLY loves them, and how He sees them as His precious daughters, His princesses . . . then maybe they wouldn't have let their boyfriend abuse them, maybe they wouldn't let their bosses call them names, maybe they wouldn't let their family speak negative words over their life . . . because they might remember this special day. They might remember that picture of their sparkly crown and that they are priceless.

Each semester after that, we had a new set of girls and it just got better and better. Each group was always unique and special. It was, and still is, one of the best things that ever happened to me. I still get just as excited as the first day we started. The number of girls who come through EG has grown every semester, but God has never given us more than we can handle.

As I serve where God has placed me, my heart is full and I feel inspired every week. Embrace Grace is not a chore or a job to me. It is a joy! Because these girls are so hungry and desperate for God to rescue them, seeking Him with their whole hearts, God comes in and shows off. I have heard so many stories of how God spoke a word, gave a dream, performed a miracle, or gave hope to each of these girls, and they are deeply etched in my heart. I have front row seats to miracles every day and I wanted to share some of the stories that have strengthened my faith in God.

I was first inspired to write this book by a girl that joined Embrace Grace during our third semester. Her name is Jordan.

⁂ *Jordan* ⁂

Jordan was nineteen years old and, like the other girls in our group, she was pregnant and unmarried. She joined the class a little late into the semester but after we heard her story, we made an exception and let her join us.

Jordan had just found out she was pregnant and was very scared. She was an only child and her mom left when she was just a baby—so it was just Jordan and her father. She also had a boyfriend.

After her dad found out about the pregnancy, he was angry and hurt, telling her she was unfit to be a mother and insisted she place the baby in an adoption program. Jordan felt conflicted; in her heart, she wanted to be a mother, but no one in her life agreed.

One day, as she tearfully drove herself to work at the UPS shipping store, she cried out to God and asked Him to send someone that could help her and show her what to do—someone in whom she could confide, and receive help. In desperation, she said, "God, just send someone today with a package that says the word *church* on it, and then I'll know it's safe for me to ask for help."

The day crawled by with lots of customers coming to her counter, but none with the word *church*. Five minutes prior to the store closing, a man came in with boxes labeled *church*! She knew it must be a sign from God.

She excitedly asked him, "Do you work at a church?" He answered, "No, I have a business that helps churches." As her heart started to sink, the man explained that he did, however, attend Gateway Church, conveniently located across the street from the store. That was all Jordan needed to hear; she knew this must be her help from God.

She poured out her heart to this stranger, explaining her pregnancy, her loved ones' reactions, and just how desperate she was for answers. The father of four listened patiently and reassured her that their church might be able to help. Before he left, the man said some encouraging words and told her he would pray for her. A few phone calls later, Jordan found herself in our little group, sitting at a table with other single and pregnant girls. As she shared her story, I saw hope in her eyes: finally, someone understood.

Jordan's story is so dear to my heart; not only how she cried out to God in her most troubled moment, or her courage to share her story with a complete stranger and ask for help, but for something she said under her breath at the very end of sharing with the class. The subtle beauty of her statement didn't hit me immediately, but it had a deep and lasting memory in my heart: *"My dad said I would be a bad mom, but that guy I met at the UPS store said he thought I would be a good mom."*

The gentleman spoke words of life into her, right there at the express mail store. He didn't say some profound and beautiful statement that should be hung on a wall somewhere; he just spoke what came out of his heart. He may not have thought twice about those words, but to Jordan, it was life to her soul.

That simple statement has changed my whole outlook on my words, and how most of these girls just need some encouragement and hope. They just need someone to believe in them, someone to say, "You're going to be a good mom. You can do this!"

There are so many that have found themselves single, pregnant, and alone, each with their own unique story. But one common feeling that they all deeply desire—and desperately need—is *hope*.

I know, because Jordan's story is my story too.

Me

I was on the floor with nurses leaning over me, fanning me and calling out my name. What had just happened?

Earlier, as I sat in the cold, sterile clinic office, a few words were ringing in my ears:

Almost seven weeks pregnant.

Abortion.

Vacuum method.

There was a pill I could take if I was six weeks pregnant or less that might make the baby "go away." I didn't really want to try to comprehend *how* the baby would just "go away," but the less I thought about it, the less frightening this situation seemed.

The nurse had interrupted my thoughts, explaining to me that I actually was too far along to take the "go-away" pill, and had shown me a pamphlet of the vacuum method and how the procedure works. My stomach overturned and the room began to spin as I tried to process everything she was saying. Her words echoed in my ears as I felt the color rush from my cheeks . . . and then the room had gone black.

A few moments later, I opened my eyes and two nurses were hovering over me, fanning me. "Amy, are you okay? You just fainted. Just take some long, deep breaths," the woman said. As I started to get my bearings straight, the nurses (slower this time) explained to me how I was too far along to take the pill, so it would be the suction method. That was all I could hear and I just started crying . . . the tears wouldn't stop.

Could I really go through with this?

I felt like I could barely breathe. The nurse stopped talking for a moment and just stared at me. She said, "You shouldn't have a procedure today. You're too emotionally distraught. You can come back another time and reschedule. But today, you are not getting an abortion." A sense of relief washed over me, which was odd since I really did not want to have a baby.

I walked back out into the waiting room where my boyfriend was waiting for me.

Looks like we're really going to do this. I'm having a baby.

Growing up in a very strict home and going to a Christian private school, I knew my family and friends were going to freak out; they might even disown me. Every worst possible scenario crossed my mind.

My boyfriend, Ryan, felt the same way. He was starting his second year of college and relied heavily on his dad for financial support. He figured his dad would cut monthly school and living allowances, and possibly even cut him off from the family. We had no idea how we could support a baby when we could barely support ourselves. We were still so young. These were supposed to be our carefree years where we stay up late and sleep all day—not late-night feedings and diaper changes.

Eventually, I found the nerve to tell my parents; they didn't freak out as much as I'd envisioned. Don't get me wrong—there were definitely tears and yelling. My mother just cried, "Why?" and asked how could this happen, while my father stayed silent, except to say, "I had a feeling." He never got emotional or mad, just quiet. I couldn't decide if his quiet reaction was better than losing his temper, but no one was more disappointed in me than me.

I wasn't disowned, nor excommunicated; they didn't kick me out of the house. Over time, they actually started to be a little excited about it; Ryan's family reacted the same way. It was a relief that this big secret weighing so heavy on us was finally out in the open.

But that's family—not friends. As news about the pregnancy spread quickly, my friends stopped calling as much. If I took the initiative to call them, hardly anyone would ever answer their phone; and if they did answer, it was just awkward . . . it was the elephant in the room. I knew they still liked me, but if the word *baby* came up, the conversation seemed to get uncomfortable. All my friends were my age; they had no idea how to react and talk to me. Should they be excited and happy? Or apologetic and sympathetic? They didn't really know, and really, I didn't know how I felt either.

I felt very alone during this season. I didn't have a girlfriend to call and talk about aches and pains or baby kicks. I couldn't call a friend to ask if something was normal for a pregnancy or not. I had my mother, but it had been a while since she had a baby so she didn't remember a whole lot. And I had my boyfriend, Ryan; he would do the normal guy thing and listen to me talking but wouldn't actually *hear* what I was saying or asking. How could he? I was the one carrying the baby.

But our relationship grew closer through all of this; somehow, all the petty stuff we normally got upset about didn't seem so important anymore. He kicked his life into high gear, doubling up on classes and working two jobs. If there was ever anything extra after bills, we would set it aside for the baby, no matter how small the amount was.

In the past, our relationship had been very up and down with typical high school drama, breaking up and then getting back together on a regular basis. We both felt deep down, however, that some day we would get married. And since we were eventually going to get married, we should just go ahead and get married. Somehow, we managed to pull off an amazing wedding in record time; at sixteen weeks, I cinched my dress up extra tight and got an extra thick girdle to hold my belly in!

Jess was born that winter, and I was no longer concerned about the sacrifices that I would make to be a young mother. I never felt like I was missing out on the wild life or not having a chance to "sow my wild oats." All I needed and wanted was my little family; but our lives changed.

For starters, things were definitely tight with our finances. We scrimped and saved every extra penny we had. I traded in my Mustang convertible for a big, old, red Pontiac Bonneville that I named "The Bomb." (It was so ugly!) Ryan finally finished college, quit his two jobs, and began his career. After Jess got a little older, we had three more kids. We put God first in our lives, which seemed to make everything fall into place. Life was different and certainly not perfect, but I was happy.

Even as we settled into the routine business of life—church, sports practices, school, and homework—I never forgot that time in my life when I had so many uncertainties and worries about my future while carrying my first baby. It was a difficult time, but a time for spiritual growth; I had never had to rely so much on my heavenly Father, and He took care of all of our needs.

I am so thankful that I didn't go through with what I had set out to do in that sterile clinic at the beginning of pregnancy. I am so thankful that I was too far along to just swallow a pill and make my sweet son just "go away." I am thankful I had a nurse that cared enough to see my heart and not let me go through with something that I would forever regret. I am thankful that I started to wake up from my trance and realized what I was doing before it was too late. I am so thankful for my baby boy.

❧ Danielle ❧

For most of my life, I had this idea of what I wanted my future to look like. I was going to follow in the footsteps of my father and be a recording artist and songwriter. I wanted to be a world-changer. My life was mapped out; nothing and no one could get in my way. While other girls my age were dreaming about who would ask them to prom, I was in my room praying for my future.

But I was, and always had been, a control freak. It was always hard for me to fully put my trust in God and surrender everything to Him. When things did not go according to plan, it stressed me out. I would break down and have panic attacks, because things weren't going my way.

Things started going downhill when my best friend stopped talking to me because of the sex, drugs, and alcohol I was using. Suddenly, I had never felt so insecure. My mom could see that my emotions were spinning out of control so she sent me to a counselor; yet things only got worse.

Once I hit my senior year in high school, depression hit. I started self-harming, and I just wanted to be alone. Painful memories resurfaced, including sexual abuse by two family friends who were girls. Soon my counselor put me on antidepressants. When I wouldn't sign a "petition" saying that I wouldn't commit suicide, I was put on 24/7 observation, meaning I could not be alone under any circumstances; this lasted for three months.

While all of my friends were making final decisions on college, all I could think about was how I wanted to hide away from the world. I decided to stay home and go to a community college. During my second semester of school, I decided living wasn't an option. My life was a joke, and all I wanted to do was escape the pain that so heavily weighed upon my heart; at the same time, I was numb—ironic, I know.

The Lord decided to spare me, which at the time was the worst thing that had ever happened to me—or so I thought. Little did I know that going through depression was like climbing over an anthill compared to what I would face a few years later.

When I was twenty-one years old, I learned that I was pregnant outside of marriage. I found out in a Wal-Mart bathroom—how lame is that? How could my life be spinning so badly out of control? How had I let myself get so far from what I had planned for myself? Wasn't I taught that sex before marriage was wrong? Hadn't my parents given me a purity ring when I was thirteen? I knew I was strong enough to face the temptation, yet when my world started spinning out of control, I caved in to the world's ways.

How was I ever going to tell my parents, my family, and my friends? What would people think of me when they saw that I was pregnant, with no wedding ring on my finger? Even with all of the things I had been through in my past, nothing made me feel more helpless in my entire life.

Both my mother and father were extremely disappointed with me regarding the choices that I had made. While each initially reacted with totally different emotional responses, in the end they sat with me and discussed the future and what that would possibly look like. It was a traumatic and very difficult process.

I had no money, no job, and no way to make an income for my baby. The father of my baby and I were no longer together, so why should I keep her? What kind of mother would I be if I were selfish enough to let my daughter live in a home where her parents weren't married? All I wanted was a way out. My parents immediately brought up adoption, not because they wanted me to give my baby up, but because they wanted me to know all of my options. I decided that was the best choice.

December 5, 2010

My heart is full with regret and remorse. Regret for the decisions I've chosen to make and remorse for the life I have to live because of those decisions. My heart, my whole being, is bitter. I'm bitter at myself for not listening to the wisdom of my elders and parents. I'm bitter with myself for not seeing that what was right in front of me was so very wrong. I'm bitter at the baby's father for not loving me enough to say no. I'm bitter for being selfish and putting myself, my wants, before my dreams and my needs. I'm so bitter that I let myself believe the lies; I let myself be this person that I never wanted to be. When you're a child, you never dream that you would make mistakes. You never would ever think your bad choices will come back to haunt you—but they do. I never wanted this for my life. I always said I would never be that person, and now look at me. I'm living my own personal nightmare. I'm having a baby with a man who doesn't care about me. I'm unwed and pregnant and soon the world will know that I had sex before marriage.

I was so wrapped up in the *whys* that I didn't focus on anything else. I finally wasn't in control of something, and it petrified me. I made everyone think that the Lord told me to give my baby away, when in actuality I just wanted to escape. After all, that's what I was best at doing. That's all I ever knew; that's how I got through life, by escaping my problems. As soon as I had my baby, I would simply start over.

It complicated things a tad bit that my father was not only a pastor, but also part of the well-known Christian group Phillips, Craig, and Dean. I was terrified that as soon as his congregation found out that I was pregnant, they would leave his church. I would only be able to hide my growing belly for a little while longer. People were already starting to talk.

One Sunday morning, my father decided to put the rumors to rest. He said, "Danielle, if people want to leave my church because you got pregnant outside of marriage, then I don't want them at my church." He told his congregation that I was, indeed, pregnant. And not only was I pregnant, but I was going to give my baby up for adoption. I felt guilty that he was the one who had to share my mistake.

Then he told me what happened next.

The entire church stood up and starting applauding. They weren't applauding my father—they were applauding *me*! How could people who barely knew me support my sin? After the service, dozens and dozens of people came up to my father and showered him with encouragement.

Six months into my pregnancy, I started feeling a connection with my baby. All of a sudden, I didn't feel so alone anymore; I started questioning whether or not adoption was still the right choice. For a week, I prayed for the Lord to show me what *He* wanted me to do; but all He told me was, "You're going to be a great mother." I heard it in my heart as well as from the most unlikely sources.

Near the end of my pregnancy, I got an e-mail from my brother—the e-mail came just as I was feeling a tugging in my heart, little whispers from God, that my baby girl was mine.

> *I want to assure you that this baby would be a blessing to our family and not a curse. I understand that you feel like giving the baby up for*

adoption might give it more consistency and a better chance for the future and all of that stuff . . . but if you are really serious about it, let's be honest: There is a unit that surrounds you now that none of us would trade for the world. What kind of an environment could a child be raised in emotionally and spiritually right now that would be better than this one? I can't think of many. Again, these are my thoughts only. I don't expect anything from you in the way of a response and my support will not change for you either way. I just wanted you to know my thoughts. I believe you to have all the resources you need to make this work. I believe you can do this and you are set up for success to make it happen.

Two questions as I end:

1) Does God make mistakes?

2) Does God put more on your plate than you can handle?

After having several similar confirmations, I decided that this baby girl was mine after all, and I allowed myself to love her. I stopped focusing on my future, and started planning for hers—ours. I stopped living my life in fear of what might have been, and I started trusting that God would take care of my baby and me.

April 18, 2011

Well, I'm keeping my beautiful baby girl! Her name is going to be Sailor Promise. I talked with a bunch of people and they all support me. I want to raise her. I want to love and care for her and heal her boo-boos. I want to watch her grow up and get married!!! I want to go shopping with her! I love this life inside of me, and yes, it's going to be hard. There are going to be days when I want to give up, but I trust that the Lord will provide if I do my part. I love you, Sailor!

To God Be the Glory,

Danielle Dean

Telling my family and friends that I was keeping my baby would be extremely difficult and embarrassing. I felt like I was always explaining myself, arguing with people that the Lord was really leading me to adoption. But like I stated previously, He really wasn't.

My parents were the first people I told; they had no expressions on their faces. All they said was, "Okay, we support you." I was so hurt by their reactions. I then started calling different people and telling them; I even posted it on Facebook. For some reason, I thought people were going to be angry with me; instead, the response was quite positive.

A couple of weeks after the news about me keeping my baby became official, my dad made an announcement at church. It happened again but this time, the applause was even bigger and louder.

The church rose to their feet applauding my decision—and me? I never really looked at the situation as something to applaud. I did not have a baby within the covenant of marriage . . . but it was the choices I made *after the fact* that made people applaud. I could have had an abortion, and kept it a secret my entire life. I started thinking, maybe I don't have to be so hard on myself. Maybe I can live my life knowing that I *saved* a life.

Sailor Promise was born soon after. God had taught me more in the previous thirty-seven weeks than I think I've ever learned in my whole life. He taught me how to love someone I have never even met. He taught me patience and perseverance. He taught me that I am a fighter and a selfless person; that when I put my mind to something, I can accomplish anything I want.

God taught me how to fully rely on Him, because when I was pregnant that's all I could do. Most important, He taught me how to release control and let *Him* take the reins. I am never fully going to be in control of a situation, and for the first time in my life, I am *okay* with that! Nothing is too big for God.

But I think the biggest thing that I learned is God's love for mankind. I thought I knew what love was until I saw Sailor for the first time. *Love* is a word that is used every day, but it is a sacred word to me now; I don't use it lightly. Now that I have Sailor, I realize how much God loves me, and how He truly gave His life for me. He lived a perfect life, yet He got ridiculed and died a terrible, grueling death, and if I were the only person in the world, He would die just for me. I never understood that kind of love until Sailor was born.

My life may not be ideal. I may not live in a house with a white picket fence, but I wouldn't trade anything for my sweet baby girl. Although my actions were a sin, Sailor turned out to be the biggest blessing ever. When I go to any church, whether my father's or the one I attend, Gateway, no one ever gives me a dirty look. I can't go anywhere without someone complimenting Sailor. And if someone does give me a dirty look, I just smile and think to myself, "I am a daughter of the Most High King, and I rock!"

✦ *Amber* ✦

I never thought it would happen to me.

I had an amazing boyfriend who hung the moon. I was a junior in high school, a girl from a small town in Georgia. Everything was perfect—until my whole world came crashing down.

I have never wanted anything more than to be a mother. I knew I was great with children, and while I knew there were lots of ways I wasn't ready for this, I was willing to give up everything for my child.

I didn't grow up in a tight-knit household. My dad raised my sister and me, and as a man, he really had no clue how to talk to girls. When I told him, he didn't say much. When I told my Nana (his mother, who has played the role of my mother my whole life), she wasn't mad, just disappointed. That hurt worse than everything else.

And when I told my "amazing" boyfriend I was pregnant, he cussed me up and down, repeatedly saying I should have an abortion. I had just turned seventeen, and really didn't know much about abortions, except for what it meant would happen to the baby. I told him I wouldn't have one. He could leave me, but I was having the baby with or without him.

And then my own father gave me the same advice. My whole world came crashing down again. Here was the only man that I knew truly loved me, telling me to do the same thing advised by the boy whom I thought loved me. I told him no; I had more respect than that for myself and for God.

When my dad kicked me out, I booked a flight to Texas that night to stay at my aunt Angel's. After letting my father know I'd arrived, I didn't speak to my father for months.

Angel had some friends from church who had been trying to have a baby for a long time. She asked me if I had considered adoption, and would I be willing to just have dinner with them; I agreed. They were the sweetest people in the world, and I fell in love with them.

I have never been super close with God; I knew that in a hard time like this, He would take me under His wing. So I prayed, asking, *Do I keep this baby? Do I have an abortion? Or do I go through with adoption?*

For some reason, I heard a voice in my head say, "Amber, this is not your baby. Your day will come, but this baby is Shari's and Joey's." I cried and cried, but I knew what I had to do. God had spoken to me, and I knew I had to obey. I asked my aunt if we could have Shari and Joey over for dinner; when it came time for dessert, I knew I had to let them know my decision.

I looked at my aunt and uncle, then told Shari and Joey, "The Lord spoke to me, and He told me this was a baby for you." They lost it. Tears were everywhere. I was crying because it felt so right, and I had no regrets. They left that night, and I lay in my bed, praying that God would hold my hand and guide me the whole way through the process. He spoke to me again, telling me how proud He was of me and how I would continue to be blessed.

My father still wasn't happy with my decision, because it was not what he had wanted for me. My boyfriend also fussed, but I did not care; I knew God was on my side. That was also the last time I spoke to the baby's father.

A week later, I started attending a group called Embrace Grace—a group full of girls like me, who had found themselves pregnant. The girls in the group looked so scared. They looked as if they had no idea what to do—I could relate. We all became like sisters;

we helped each other, talked to each other, and made sure we were all there for each other. If it had not been for Embrace Grace, I don't think I could have made it through my pregnancy.

On October 23, I had a beautiful baby boy; Shari and Joey were with me the whole time. My aunt was there, as well as my Nana, who came from Georgia. As they were getting ready to take me to recovery, I asked Shari why she hadn't been to see her son. She told me she didn't want to leave her baby girl; she was torn between her son and the person she now thought of as her daughter. I realized that she meant me. She had come to love me as her own!

To this day, I have never seen him. I don't think I'm strong enough yet, but I know one day God will give me the strength to see him. Until then, I'll keep admiring his smiling photos and praying for him and his parents, Shari and Joey.

I'm so glad I chose life and gave him a chance at a good and happy life. He is a gift to everyone; and even though it was hard, I would never take back the journey I went through. I'm stronger because of it.

Olivia

To my beautiful baby girl,

I don't even know what to say. I've never felt so much love for someone as I do for you now. You were just born today. I can finally see you and hold you in my arms. Every worry and concern went away the moment I first saw your beautiful face. I burst into tears at the sight of your tiny hands and feet. You're mine. How incredible is that? You're my daughter! How God entrusts me with such an incredible gift makes no sense to me, but I'm so glad He did.

While I was pregnant with you, I'm not going to lie—I was scared. I mean I was "that girl," the teen mom. I was scared to face all the stares, *whispers, and challenges of being a single mom. Even with all of these worries, I was in love with you the second I found out I was pregnant.*

The thing I was most scared about was providing you a great life. How could I provide that for you? How would you grow up with an example of a godly marriage and family with me as your mom? I can't tell you that I have everything figured out even now, but I can tell you that God has everything planned and under control. Don't ever forget that, Layla. God has you in the palm of His hand. Trust in Him always.

Through all of this, I have been more in love with you than I thought possible. When I saw you today, that love grew even more. I promise to be the best mother I can possibly be. I'll be there when you're sick, when some loser breaks your heart, when you get an A+ on your spelling test, and any other time. I will always be here. I'll be the arms to crawl in when you're hurt and I'll be your biggest fan through your whole life. I'll make many mistakes as your mom and I know I won't always be your favorite person, but you'll always be mine.

I can't wait to see the amazing plans God has for you. I pray your relationship with Him is close, real, and intimate. I pray you'll know His grace and mercy.

You're my love. You are so incredibly beautiful. You're my life. I'm so excited for this journey as mother and daughter we'll be taking together.

I love you so much, my beautiful baby Layla.

Love, Mommy

❧ *Amanda* ☙

  Amanda found out she was pregnant in her jail cell.

By then, her life had spiraled out of control—she was strung out, homeless, and unemployed. She used anything she could to try and fill the vast emptiness inside and numb the painful memories of her past. Men, drugs, alcohol, money . . . they all left her still starving.

Struggling with deep depression, she found herself at a hospital and couldn't remember why or how she got there. The nurses told her that she had tried to take her own life by swallowing two bottles of pills. The foggy memory of it all was slowly coming back to her as she lay in her hospital bed. She hated her life and needed an escape—but her plan hadn't worked.

God had a different plan.

And only two weeks later, she ended up in jail. She had good intentions of paying the tickets but could never keep a job long enough to have any extra money. The tickets eventually turned to warrants, and Amanda was arrested. Why had her life turned out like this?

Amanda assumed the vomiting and nausea was due to the depression and fear, but the warden suggested a pregnancy test. Two minutes later, it was confirmed— she was pregnant.

Amanda had been living with her mother since she was thirteen years old and had watched her struggle with a lot of the same addictions that she herself had. When Amanda telephoned her mother and whispered the words out loud for the first time, her mother called her a liar and hung up on her.

A few days later, Amanda was released. Heading straight to the local free pregnancy clinic to see if maybe this was just all some big mistake, she called her mother and asked her to meet her there. She needed someone, anyone, even someone who thought she was a liar. She couldn't do this alone.

When Amanda arrived at the clinic, she was thankful to see her mother already there. She knew she was angry, but at least she showed up. As the nurse moved the transducer over Amanda's belly, she could see the tiny form of a baby. Amanda felt overwhelmed. At the nurse's instruction, Amanda used the restroom so they could get a clearer picture. When Amanda returned, her mom was gone. According to the nurses, she had walked out the door, saying, "Screw this, I'm going home."

Amanda's heart broke. She was alone.

And since the father of the baby was a drug addict, Amanda only had one other person she could turn to—her own father. She had only seen him four times in the last four years. He had a family with younger kids, and he didn't want Amanda's lifestyle to be a negative influence on their lives. But now, maybe things would be different. Since she was pregnant, she really wasn't even craving the drugs or alcohol anymore. Even the thought of a cigarette made her gag.

She dialed his number and said the dreaded words again: "I'm pregnant." He said, "You've got to be kidding me! I'll call you back," and then hung up. Three long days later, he called her back, inviting her over to their house for the weekend so they could talk. She wondered if that meant he could yell at her face to face, but she had been so lonely, she didn't care.

Except that he didn't yell. Instead, her dad asked her to move in with the family so that they could help her. He wanted her to have a stable home to live in that was a healthy and happy environment. She was starting to see a glimmer of hope as the knowledge that she was really going to have a baby became more and more real.

She began to ask questions about her traumatic past. Where was God when all the bad things happened to her? She struggled with believing He was real, much less that He loved her. But over the course of the next few months, she really started to open up and seek Him. Her heart was starting to open up a little more each time we saw her at Embrace Grace.

Climbing into bed one night, Amanda pondered all sorts of questions. *Is there really a God? And does He really love me like they were saying? Could He love me after all that I've done?* She closed her eyes and whispered out loud, "If You're real, and You're really there and You hear me, will You give me a sign or a dream or something so I know? I just don't know what to believe or think anymore. I need a sign. Please show me that You're there." A few minutes later, she drifted off to sleep and had a dream.

The dream began with Amanda painting what seemed to be the bedroom that she would be sharing with the baby—there was a small crib in the corner and her bed on the other side of the room. She had a paintbrush in her hand and was dipping it into bright colors of pink and purple paint, transforming the walls from stark white to beautiful, vibrant hues. She then painted beautiful butterflies over the crib, some big and some small. The room looked so cheery and sweet. For the first time, she felt a sense of peace and happiness as she took in the result of all her hard work, seeing the room complete.

The dream then changed scenes.

She was in her bathroom at her dad's house, sitting on the edge of the bathtub, doubled over in pain. She realized that her contractions were steady—and were getting closer together and more intense. She knew it was time: this baby was coming. So many thoughts were engulfing her mind. *Will I be a good mother? What if something bad happens when I have her? Can I provide for my baby and be able to take care of all the needs?*

At that point, Amanda yelled to her sister, "Go get my dad, the baby is coming! I'm scared! Tell him to help me! I need help and I don't know if I have the strength to do this! Please help me!" When her father entered the bathroom, he said, "It's okay. I'm here. Everything is going to be okay. Don't be afraid. We're going to get through this. I'll be right here with you. Just trust me." Then, Amanda woke up.

It was only 5:00 a.m., so Amanda stayed in bed to process her dream. She thought about the butterflies over the crib and the bright colors. *Why would I have painted that when I don't even know if I am having a boy or girl yet? The dream got so intense but at the end, my dad made me feel so much better.* Amanda's eyes were getting heavy again. As she closed her eyes she thought, *Could that have been God?* As she drifted back to sleep she quietly said, "God, was that You?"

A few moments later, she was in a deep sleep and had the *same dream.* Scene by scene, word for word, all over again. It went from painting the butterflies to the bathroom, doubled over in pain. Her father arrived, helped her up, and said those comforting words.

When she woke up a few hours later, she thought to herself how crazy to have the same dream twice in one night! As she processed it, Amanda realized that the second dream was different. . . . It started out just like before, but this time when her father spoke, Amanda realized that *her father's mouth was not moving.* The voice was a strong, deep male voice that filled the room and penetrated her soul. It seemed familiar, but she knew she'd never heard it before. The voice had so much strength, depth, and power, yet gave her an indescribable peace. The words sank into her heart: *"It's okay. I'm here. Everything is going to be okay. Don't be afraid. We're going to get through this. I'll be right here with you. Just trust Me."*

As tears filled her eyes, the same question resurfaced:

"God, was that You?" Deep down, she already knew the answer.

The next day, Amanda excitedly told me about her dream and we immediately began researching what the meaning of butterflies was: *New creation, new life, new beginnings.* When we ask God into our lives and are "born again," we are a "new creation." Amanda was definitely walking into a season of new life and new beginnings.

Over the next few months, Amanda had SO many butterfly stories! She found butterfly jewelry on the street, butterflies in her car, butterflies flying all around her. God began to woo her with His love. She found out she was pregnant with a baby girl and designed her nursery as it had been in her dreams—with butterflies.

Later that October, she gave her life to Jesus. She could not deny Him anymore, believing with all her heart that He was her Lord and Savior. She now lives confidently and trusts with all her heart that God will always take care of her and her baby girl.

༄ Jordyn ༄

When I met Jordyn, she was pregnant with a baby girl. Every time I saw her, she was talking about her baby. She proudly showed off her sonogram photos to anyone that she could, and she loved hearing her baby's heartbeat and talking about her doctor appointments. She updated me on her baby's growth *in utero* and how her baby was developing. When her baby would kick, she would grab my hands and put them on her belly. She loved throwing out ideas for her baby's first and middle name to see what her friends' thoughts were. Her heart was filled with anticipation and excitement just like every momma does during her pregnancy . . . but her situation was a little different than most.

Jordyn was only sixteen years old. With long blonde hair swept up in a messy ponytail, sparkly green eyes, and braces, this tiny girl had the cutest baby bump. The top button of her jeans was open to relieve her growing belly, and she was smiling. When she spoke, her ponytail bounced around like a little girl's. She was bubbly and always full of joy, even though she knew her life was about to completely change. Jordyn had made a brave and courageous decision to place her baby up for adoption.

I thought I would be mentoring her; over the course of the next five months, however, I would be the one who was profoundly, and irrevocably, impacted.

During this season of roller-coaster emotions, her strength never wavered. She struggled with horrible morning sickness and acid reflux; even brushing her teeth made her nauseous. Her pregnancy kept her lethargic and sleepy, but she pushed even harder in high school to graduate faster. She gave up her homecoming, prom, and all the usual fun teenage memories, sacrificing them to take the time she needed to prepare for this baby girl that was on her way.

Jordyn spent a lot of time, thoughts, and prayers on finding the perfect family to raise her daughter. She wanted them to be in love with Jesus, have the same morals and values that she had, have soft, sweet temperaments—and be in favor of an open adoption. After a lot of research, God brought her the perfect family. When she met them, she immediately felt at peace that they were the ones to raise her baby girl. She knew God had chosen them out of all the families in the world to be baby Abby's adoptive family.

Once she made her choice, she started collecting old baby pictures of herself and the father of the baby. She spent hours placing them all in a beautiful scrapbook, adding sonogram pictures and monthly photos of her growing belly. Jordyn hoped this would be a reminder for her baby of just how much her birth parents loved her.

Baby Abby arrived in May 2011. Overwhelmed with joy, Jordyn cried when she laid eyes on her beautiful baby girl for the first time. She told me that baby Abby was her everything and how much she was in love with her—more than anything or anyone else in her life.

In Texas, there is a law that adoption papers can't be signed any sooner than forty-eight hours after birth, so Jordyn worked out a plan with the hospital. She had reserved a hospital room for the adoptive family to be right next door to her. Jordyn got to spend the days with baby Abby, loving on her and kissing her sweet face; then at night, she wheeled the baby next door so that the adoptive family could love on her too.

After forty-eight hours, Jordyn and Abby were released from the hospital. They had a caravan of both birth and adoptive family members following each other to a special ceremony. That memory is forever sealed on my heart.

We all met at our church. Jordyn, Abby, and the baby's father were in one room, signing the papers to give this baby a better life; the next room was full of friends and family members, there to support both families. Once the papers were signed, Jordyn held baby Abby, weeping with overwhelming emotion as a pastor prayed and dedicated the baby to the Lord. When the prayer was finished, it was time to place this special treasure, this priceless jewel of Jordyn's, into God's hands. I will never forget the changing of hands, that moment when she gave everything to God. It was the most beautiful act of love I had ever encountered. She then gave the adoptive family her sweet scrapbook that she had lovingly spent hours on, making it perfect. They loved every page of it.

The days following were difficult for Jordyn. After all, she had sacrificed her body for nine months to save this baby's life, and she loved her with all her heart. The pregnancy had consumed her life, thoughts, and actions, and Abby had been a part of her physically; now, they had been separated. As her body was healing, she worked through every doubt, fear, and aching of her heart by clinging to God's Word and to what she knew God had called her to do:

A *big* love. A *deep* love. A *sacrificial* love.

Walking this journey with Jordyn, God showed me how He sees adoption. In Exodus 1 and 2, God had blessed the Israelites with many babies and their population grew rapidly. The king of Egypt felt threatened by their numbers and worried that they could overtake his throne, so he ordered all the baby boys to be drowned in the Nile River. After the ruling was made, a woman named Jochebed gave birth to a baby boy whom she knew was special. She tried her best to hide him from Pharoah's army for three months; eventually, she realized she couldn't get away with it any longer. Before placing him in the handmade basket, she actually had to *do* it—have that one last kiss, one more hug. Then, she released her priceless treasure, her everything, with one last prayer to God: *Protect my baby from harm. Save my baby.* Release. Trust. Cry. Lean. Hope. In order to save her baby's life, she had to let him go.

Most of us know the rest of the story. Pharaoh's daughter found baby Moses in the basket and God rewarded Jochebed for her obedience by making her his nurse. When he was a little bigger, Moses went to live in the Pharaoh's palace; he eventually led the Israelites out of slavery and bondage, saving the entire nation from destruction.

Moses' life changed the world; but what would have happened if Jochebed had not released him to God?

Big love is not replete of big pain. Jordyn's heart has healed more and more after releasing Abby to the adoptive family—but it's still a process. She has an open adoption, so they have scheduled visits every few months; Jordyn counts down the days till she gets to kiss her sweet Abby.

One of the ways we honor Embrace Grace mothers who choose adoption is with a big "Celebration of Life" shower. A few weeks after they give birth and bless another family with their baby, we gather all her family and friends together, along with Embrace Grace classmates and alumni, and shower her with new clothes, cute jewelry, lotions, gift cards, money, etc.; but more important, we shower her with words of love.

The best part of the party occurs when every guest picks out a unique bead from a big glass bowl—they are all different sizes, shapes, colors, and textures— that reminds them of the guest of honor. (Even if they haven't met her, they choose a bead inspired by her story.) We take a long string and pass it around the room; each person strings the bead, while sharing what it means: red heart for the sacrifice made, a pearl for the refined beauty that now shines through, and so on. The birth mother then has a necklace that reminds her of her love, her life, and those who love her in return.

Jordyn has found a new determination to make something of herself, and to walk alongside girls who are in similar situations; as a young leader in Embrace Grace, she shares her story with transparency—reflecting on who she was before, where she is now, and how God was with her throughout the entire journey. Countless women have been touched and inspired by the selfless act of this young sixteen-year-old girl. What she has been through in her short life can only be a story that God uses for His glory.

Having had a front row seat to the miracles in Jordyn's life, I can bear witness that this kind of love is *huge* to me, yet still serves as only a reflection of how much my God loves me and you. What have I learned from Jordyn? To *love* big.

Heather

Heather became a Christian at a young age, but her memories were not warm and fuzzy. Her years growing up in church had given her the idea that God was stern, judgmental, and punishing. She had been taught, and believed, that you had to do things perfectly; otherwise, God would punish you and you would go to hell. Her warped view of God made it hard to keep living the life of striving for perfection, so why try?

After losing her grandmother to breast cancer, Heather was incensed when her mother was diagnosed too. She was mad at God for letting her mom have cancer and didn't understand what her mom did to deserve such a cruel sickness. Heather was only twelve, and couldn't understand why her family could be separated from her forever at a time when she needed them most.

In spite of her illness, Heather's mother agreed to teach Vacation Bible School. One day, just before singing a patriotic song, the pastor asked everyone to remove their hats out of respect. Heather's mom had just started losing her hair to chemotherapy, so she didn't take her hat off. Someone yelled out a rude comment; Heather looked at her mom and cringed, feeling so bad and embarrassed for her. She thought, *How could that man say that to my mother at a time like this? Does he not know how much she is going through right now?* That was the last straw for Heather. She had had enough of God and church. Heather and her mom quit going to church as often after that incident, and eventually just stopped going altogether. For Heather, blaming God was easier than coping with the situation in a healthy way.

When her mother was finally declared cancer-free, however, Heather had already begun the downward spiral of living out her life her own way and running away from God at every turn.

Throughout high school, Heather consistently found herself in trouble. She was arrested for truancy and was in and out of detention constantly. In college, she moved to hard drugs and partying. Eventually, she made the wise decision to come back home before she developed addictions that would be too hard to break.

She met Jason a few months after moving home, and they started dating. Although she wasn't as wild as she had been at the university, she was still drinking heavily almost every day and she spent more and more time with Jason. During that time, Heather and her roommate's monthly cycles were usually "synched up." One week, her friend ended her cycle and Heather realized she still had not started yet. At first, she didn't think much of it; then she noticed that every time she smoked, she would get really nauseous and could never finish her cigarette. Her breasts were getting much bigger, and when her mother overheard her boasting to a friend about growing a cup size, she suggested that Heather might want to take a pregnancy test.

Despite her symptoms, Heather still didn't think there was any way it could be true. She took the test just to put her mother at ease, and was completely shocked to find a little plus sign in the window. Surely it had to be wrong! Maybe the test was expired? Maybe it's a false positive? Maybe she was misreading the results?

It was for real. Heather was pregnant.

She already had a game plan, though—long ago, she had made the decision that if she ever got pregnant accidentally, she would have an abortion. It was the only option that could work for her.

She called Jason to let him know the news and he agreed that abortion was the best option for them. There was just no way it made sense that either one could be a parent at this point. She was only nineteen years old after all—her life was just getting started.

Still, Heather was a whirlwind of emotions. *How could I have gotten myself into this mess? How could I have been so careless and gotten pregnant? I am nineteen years old, I know better than this! Why does this have to happen? I wish this would all just go away. I don't want an abortion and I don't want a baby. I just want this nightmare to be over!* She cried all day long every day as she waited for *the* appointment. She wanted to get it all over with.

With her ex-boyfriend and her mom along for support, Heather's anxiety level was at an all-time high as she approached the abortion clinic. As they slowly turned the corner toward the facility, she saw a crowd of pro-life picketers all standing on the curb with signs. They weren't the ugly mean activists with their grotesque pictures, ranting and raving. It seemed to be a peaceful group, standing quietly and holding signs that said things like, "Pray for the babies," "Life is beautiful," and "You're not alone."

Heather's heart sank as she drove past the people to

get to the parking lot. Tears spilled over her cheeks and she froze. She couldn't get out of the car. Jason and her mom kept trying to talk her into going inside, but she just couldn't do it. She couldn't stop crying. She felt so many emotions but she couldn't put even one of them into words. She couldn't try to make them understand when she didn't even understand herself. She just wasn't ready.

They scheduled their second appointment, and apologized to clinic staff for being a "no show." They would definitely make it to the next one. They wanted to take care of the matter before she got too far along.

The second time, there were no picketers outside. Heather breathed a sigh of relief and slowly made her way inside. The clinic felt cold and sterile. She looked around the waiting room and saw other girls about her age. They all seemed uneasy. Some were nervously checking their cell phones; some were chewing on their fingernails or tapping their pens on the clipboard. Her heart was broken, and it felt like she could barely put one foot in front of another. Her nerves were shot, and she hadn't slept in days.

She sat down into the stiff chair as her mother checked her into the front desk. Heather joined the rest of the girls in filling out all the necessary paperwork as her mother paid the balance due for the procedure. The first page was a medical release form for an abortion. It said that an abortion is "the termination of pregnancy by the removal or expulsion from the uterus of a fetus or embryo prior to viability." That didn't sound so bad, did it? *I'm just having the fetus removed before it's viable.* Heather took a deep sigh as a tear dropped down her cheek again. *Why is this happening to me?* The nurse interrupted Heather's thoughts as her name was called out in the waiting room.

Following another pregnancy test to confirm her pregnancy, the nurse reviewed Heather's medical history forms and asked a series of questions. She stopped when she noticed that Heather had checked off "seizures" on her form.

As a child, Heather would frequently have seizures but thanks to medication, she had not had an episode in many years. Regardless, she would need a medical release from her regular doctor approving and signing off on the abortion procedure, as Heather would now require general anesthesia due to her history of seizures. The nurse asked Heather to go back to the waiting room while they waited on the form to be sent back from her doctor.

Minutes turned into hours, giving Heather enough time to resolve, *When this is over, I'm going to start over*

*with a clean slate. I'm going to make some big changes in
my life. Things will be different.*

The nurse walked out to the waiting room and interrupted Heather's thoughts. The form had arrived, but
it was too late in the day now to actually perform the
procedure so they would have to reschedule for another
day. Heather, her mother, and Jason left in frustration
having scheduled a third appointment for the only available opening—on Christmas Eve. They rode home in
silence, though Heather was disappointed that she had
scheduled a Christmas memory that she would carry for
the rest of her life . . . the Christmas that she "termi-
nated her pregnancy."

When Heather arrived for her third and final
appointment, the nurse escorted her back quickly. She
was still struggling with her nerves but knew this was
still the only option that made sense. She had to get this
abortion and then move forward, putting all this pain
behind her.

Once in her gown, she went into a holding area
where she had to watch an informational video about
the procedure. She listened to the first few minutes as
they talked about recovery times and all the aftercare
instructions. She tried to pay attention but her stomach
was doing flip-flops and she just couldn't listen to the

words. There was no way she could concentrate, so she turned the volume down and closed her eyes.

Why am I even here? I want to be anywhere else but here at this moment. I want to pretend this isn't happening and just leave. If I ignore it, will it go away? Of course not. I have to do this! It will be over in just a few minutes. Why am I even here for the third time? It should have happened the first time I made an appointment but random things happened. . . . Was it random?

The video came to an end, and Heather was taken into the procedure room. As Heather reclined on the cold, icy table, the doctor entered the room; it was obvious he wasn't the chatty type. As the doctor reviewed Heather's charts, the nurse explained to her what was about to happen, speaking in a calm voice to relieve any of the nerves that Heather was feeling . . . but it wasn't working. Heather's heart felt like it was going to beat out of her chest. The nurse continued to point out how they were going to start an IV of general anesthesia into her arm and that within just a few seconds she would not feel anything.

Heather had feared needles her entire life. She would always do what she could to avoid having to get a shot or have any blood taken . . . but there was no getting around the IV. At least by being asleep, the thoughts in her head would stop.

Heather took a deep breath and held it as the nurse slowly slid the needle into her vein. Heather gradually let out her breath as tears filled her eyes again. She knew she was seconds away from this horrible dream being over. As the nurse reached around to grab the tape to hold the needle in place, the IV slid back out. The nurse noticed it and was baffled. She spoke quietly to the doctor and then apologized to Heather saying, "I'm very sorry, but apparently the needle has slid back out of your arm. Let's try this again. I'm so sorry."

Heather's mind started racing. *How can a needle just slide out of my arm? God, why is this so hard? Is this a sign? I can't do this! There is no way this is an accident! Three times I've tried to do this? I just can't do it!*

Heather sat straight up from the table and started crying even harder. "I can't do this anymore! I don't know why but I just can't!"

The doctor quietly slid out of the room without saying a word as the nurse talked it out with Heather. She said, "You know you don't have to do this if you don't want to."

She still didn't know if she was making the right decision; all she knew was that she could not go through with an abortion. She walked back out of the waiting room with the nurse and told Jason that she couldn't do it. His eyes narrowed as he quietly gathered his things and made his way out to the car. She could tell he was angry and that he was restraining himself, but she knew it was just a matter of time; he was about to unleash his anger.

Jason had not told his parents yet—nor did he want to. He wanted this problem to just go away, but Heather was not cooperating. He had spent hours at the abortion clinic over the past month waiting for her to get an abortion and she was *still* pregnant. What a waste of time! He started yelling and just couldn't stop. He had enough. He kept getting louder and louder. She cringed, as he was cursing her name and driving recklessly, way over the speed limit. He pounded his fist into the steering in frustration with every point he made.

Once the initial shock had worn off, reality began to set in. Heather accepted that she was going to be a mother. She started panicking less, but depression sank in quickly. She cried herself to sleep every night.

Jason moved to Florida for a job opportunity during the pregnancy, and the distance seemed to make their relationship even more disconnected. When he finally returned home, he wasted no time in finding another girl to date. It was the worst feeling in the world to be pregnant with a baby whose father was dating someone else.

Halfway through the pregnancy, Heather had her

first spark of joy when she found out she was having a girl. Even with being scared, hurt, and ashamed throughout the pregnancy, the news of having a girl planted a little seed of hope in her heart that jump-started a new thought process.

Maybe I could be a single mom and everything wouldn't be ruined. Maybe I could still achieve my dreams while having a baby on my hip. Maybe I could still meet a dream husband and he would accept my baby girl as his own. Maybe there is hope for my future yet. Maybe all of this isn't the end of my life. . . . Yes things will be different, but maybe not that bad?

Heather was in labor fourteen hours before the doctor decided her body was too small to fit the baby through the birth canal, and that she needed a C-section. Baby Emily was born weighing eight pounds, nine ounces. Looking into the eyes of her daughter, and as tired and stressed out about everything as she was, Heather wasn't prepared for how much she could love another human being. Emily was just perfect; her hands, her toes, her face . . . she was an amazing miracle. Even though she had a million things to worry about with the paternity test, custody issues, etc., Heather just knew everything was going to be okay.

When Emily was about six months old, Heather was invited to our church group called Embrace Love. Due to her past church experiences, she was reluctant and skeptical, but she was clinging to any hope she could find while going through custody battles, so she was willing to give us a try. It wasn't long before the doubts emerged, however.

Is this another church that is going to judge me and my past? Are they going to snub their nose at me because I am a young and single mom and tell me I am going to hell or something?

Before she could even take a few steps into the church building, a lady with a smile on her face walked up to her and offered to carry the baby carrier for her. Heather was surprised, but agreed. The lady grabbed it and walked alongside her as they made their way to the free meal Gateway offers single families. Heather needed to feed Emily first, and just as she reached for a bottle, one of the pastors walked up to her and offered to feed the baby so Heather could go through the line and eat her dinner. She thought, *Are these people for real?*

When class started, she met a roomful of young mothers close to her age. They had similar concerns, struggles, and even praises. *All these moms seem just like me! All these leaders and pastors seem like they don't see my sin, they just see me.*

Heather made it a weekly routine to go to Embrace Love on Monday nights. When she left church, she always felt a little lighter and she could breathe easier. There was hope and for the first time, she thought that maybe she could achieve the dreams that God had for her. Maybe she could still use these talents that God had given her after all.

Things began to fall into place. Every financial fear, every question about school—namely, how she could be a mother and go to school at the same time—God lined up the answer. He took care of everything—even the custody issues.

Today, Jason is a great father. Even though Heather and Jason are not together in a relationship, they co-parent in a respectful way. He pays child support and plays an active role as father in Emily's life, forever thankful that Heather was the stronger one those three times at the clinic. She stood up for his baby's life when he had a moment of weakness.

If that needle had just stayed in for just a few more seconds, Heather would have fallen asleep and not been able to stop the procedure . . . and they would have missed out on their life with their precious Emily.

God gave them three signs that He was going to work everything out and that this baby's life had a purpose and destiny. He gave them signs that He was going to take care of it all, and to just believe and trust Him, even though they both couldn't see past next week, much less nine months in front of them—and beyond. They didn't know how everything was going to work out, but Heather was courageous enough to take a step of faith and say, "You know, I have no idea what I'm doing or how I'm going to do it but what I do know is that I can't have an abortion. This baby will have a chance at life."

Telling her story at Embrace Grace, Heather stood at the front of the classroom looking intently into the girls' eyes as she completed telling her story. She noticed that most of the single and pregnant girls blinked back tears as they hung on to her every word. Each word spoken was hope to their soul, as if they were thinking, *If this girl can do it, maybe I can too. Maybe God will take care of me and my baby too.*

Heather closed by explaining, "It took me a while to realize just how strategically God planned my life out, and to see that He allowed my life, even with my failures and my mistakes, to so perfectly draw me back to Him. And in doing that, He gave me the best gift I could ever get—my sweet baby girl. In a way, as mad as I was, and as adamant as I was against Him, I still felt like I never completely let Him go. I think it was more of a reunion, but a much better one. I had a much better understanding of who He is, and how much He loves me.

"He doesn't care how many mistakes I have made

or all the bad things I've done. I don't have to be perfect. He wants my broken, mistake-ridden, messed-up self—He just wants me. His timing was perfect; and if you just trust in Him, your whole outlook is so much brighter, bigger, and better."

Jacqueline

Scars are usually a reminder of former trauma, whether they are faint from minor scrapes and burns, or so prominent that they seem to dominate you. The kind that overshadow the beauty of the body they disfigure, scars that suffocate the life beneath their brand. I had one of those, and a despicable pain resonated within my gut with every glance at the monstrosity overtaking my body. Little did I know as it formed that the cause of the wound had begun much earlier in my life.

My childhood was fairly mundane. I had a single mother and a brother five years my senior. I never met my father, and I recall only realizing or caring much about his lack of presence a handful of times within my sixth grade year. Those few times cut deeply, though, far deeper than I could have imagined at the innocent age of twelve.

My mother worked three jobs, so many mornings she had to drop me at school long before class began. I would sit in the cafeteria with a few other early arrivers until the bell rang, allowing us to scurry down the hallway to our classrooms. One of these early mornings the entire elementary student body was invited to Doughnuts with Dad. So there I was, gawking for an agonizing hour and fifteen minutes as every single child feasted on delicious doughnuts with their daddies. I chalk that up as my first realization my heart craved some kind of fatherly affection.

The second time occurred when I was left standing alone in the middle of an enormous ballroom dance floor surrounded by 199 of my closest peers and 400 or more of our parents on a night of cotillion. "Parents' Night" existed to demonstrate the fancy dance moves we had attained after six weeks of etiquette classes, or so I thought. To my dismay, the instructor asked us to partner with our parent of the opposite sex and dance with them, practicing what we had learned. That meant boys with their mothers, and girls with their fathers.

I stood there humiliated, surrounded by a sea of six hundred judgmental onlookers, as a woman forcefully shoved her husband out of the crowd to adopt me as his charity case of the night, while she danced with their son. Again I felt it—that gut-wrenching pain churning within my body as I choked back a waterfall of tears. Everyone already pitied the "poor girl without a dad." There was no way I would give them tears to pity as well.

Once I shed a few precious tears in private, I quickly regained composure and proceeded with my comfortable, ordinary life. Middle school, high school, and my first year of college passed quickly and successfully, with no major life-changing, "fatherless-heartache" events during those years.

I had just turned nineteen and entered my second year of college classes, and lived with my mother in a comfortable little apartment. I was pursuing my dream of becoming a second grade teacher, hoping to eventually marry a great-looking man, and have precious little babies with him. We would be a sweet whole family, with one mommy and one daddy, living happily ever after. Life was looking rather exciting and quite promising. Then along came a giant, skin-curdling, spider, with a greedy appetite and carnivorous plot.

He had just moved in across the hall from my mom and me. Vince was seven years older than me and a smooth-talking, smooth-moving ballroom dance instructor. This formerly innocent, seemingly intelligent, driven-to-succeed girl became his mindless minion within three weeks' time, and my unhealthy submission to Vince torpedoed me into a lifestyle of submission in the worst way. My heart craved the love and acceptance of this older man, so my actions carried out the robotic tasks of cleaning, cooking, and sexual gratification for him at his every beck and call. And while the love and acceptance I longed for never developed, my ability to follow orders and ask no questions certainly did.

Vince had nonchalantly told me of his petty past encounters with the law. He provided me with an unquestionably believable story explaining his wrongful conviction for the silly, innocent crime his friends had dared him to commit years ago. My desire to accept and extend grace to all people, regardless of their past, along with his manipulative way with words, overshadowed any doubt about his story. I had yet to notice that the scab over my painful daddy memories had already begun cracking open and oozing, all over my life. All the while, this man poked and prodded at my heart, using my life and my body as he pleased. And my naive loyalty to him continued.

Then, after a mere three months of knowing Vince, came the kicker to rip away the scab entirely. Thousands of thoughts whirled through my mind as I fixated on the two pink lines, but only one word stood out: *Pregnant*. I was a pregnant teenager. No matter that I'd never talked to boys until I was seventeen; I had only had one previous relationship before this toxic one; I had hopes and dreams of becoming someone wonderful . . . I was pregnant. Much to my surprise, Vince's first response was, "How much does an abortion cost in the state of Texas?"

Regardless of my nausea and throwing up multiple times a day for days on end, I continued to take orders from Vince. My formerly stable relationship with my mother began disintegrating, so eventually I shared with her the news of my pregnancy; she was distraught at first, but very quickly became a source of encouragement. She saw to it that I took care of myself, but her disdain for Vince remained—and it would be much later before I realized why.

One day, my mother suddenly locked me out of our apartment and had the locks changed; my brother arrived a couple of days later. He and my mother confronted Vince outside of our apartment doors, and my emotions were torn. My mother insisted Vince show proof to verify his past, and Vince said he had legal documents in his car that could. He went to retrieve them, and never came back.

I returned to my mother's apartment, where she directed me to a mountainous stack of papers on our coffee table. As I sat reading court documents, police reports, witness and victim statements, I read the true account of this registered sex offender's criminal history. Tears began pouring from my eyes and my heart throbbed with agony. I looked down at my expanding abdomen, at the growth overtaking my body—my scar. The disfigurement stretching from my breastbone all the way to my hips was a living, moving scar, forming over my wounded heart before my very eyes. At nineteen, I had heard my whole life how much younger I actually looked; I realized that Vince had only used me to feed his perverse appetite.

I was pregnant with a pervert's baby.

I remained vigilant in my refusal to communicate with Vince—which oddly enough, proved more difficult than I had imagined—as I watched numerous girls come and go from his apartment at all hours of the day and night. I realized my real value in this deceitful man's eyes. I was nothing special or worth saving; just a gullible little girl, longing for an older man to love her—vulnerable, appealing prey to a sexual predator.

Vince attempted a few times, via e-mail and text messages, to convince me all the reports and court documents I had read were lies. After following me to work one day, however, he left me with a final thought that echoed clearly in my mind.

"Find a new father for *that* baby!" he screamed at me, as I hurried into the building without looking back. I almost collapsed once I made it in the door, but I would not give him the satisfaction of seeing me. I had loved someone who never really existed, and I was determined to do exactly as his hateful words suggested. He would have nothing to do with the child I carried. He would never receive the opportunity to use and abuse her as he had me.

As my belly reached its maximum stretching point, I felt so ashamed of the visible brand labeling me violated, used, and disgraceful, in more ways than I could count. It wasn't until the first sunrise of February that my world would be shaken in a more wonderful way.

As I held a beautiful, flawless baby girl in my arms after a smooth cesarean section, I saw a glimmer of hope. I knew she was not a scar to remind me of a former trauma; instead, Brinley was my gift, and a promise from God of new life for the both of us.

My mother, Brinley, and I relocated to a different city and into a beautiful house, away from the spider lurking across the hall. Uncertain about all the unfamiliarity, great anticipation welled within my heart as God reminded me to dream again. I began attending church, and learning about a God of love and restoration. This God overflowed the emptiness in my heart that my earthly daddy had never filled. This God confirmed my worth and beauty; He healed my wounds and transformed my monstrous scar into a victorious princess. My life was not over because I had been a pregnant teenager; my life with my daughter had just begun to blossom.

Within seven months of my princess's birth, God blessed us with a man who saw me for the untarnished treasure I was designed to be. This man gazed upon my daughter with love, and valued her as a priceless addition. He loved her in a healthy way—a way I had never witnessed nor felt. Kyle was the really great-looking man I had dreamed of marrying so long ago; and while every memory of our time getting to know each other is precious, the moment I cherish most is when, while holding my daughter in his arms, he asked me to be his wife. He wrote his dedication as my husband in a Bible he gave me, and his dedication as Brinley's daddy in a Bible for her, a commitment he honored legally, too, having adopted her as soon as it was possible. My big little-girl dreams had at last come true—we were one family, with one mommy and one daddy, and expecting another blessing before long.

Triumph and joy now eclipse the painful memories and wounds of my past. Rather than bearing a heavy scar, I proudly tote around a hazel-eyed beauty with a glowing smile and a world of possibilities at her fingertips. While fleshly scars seem permanent, my love for my family and victory through Jesus is eternal beyond this world.

❧ *Jessica* ☙

With sore feet and an aching back, Jessica was thankful it was finally break time and she could get some relief. She was seven months pregnant, and standing all day at a fast-food drive-thru window was getting harder and harder to do. Every muscle in her body throbbed. Looking forward to a minute to just rest her back and take a deep breath, she found a quiet corner in the restaurant and sank into her chair.

Sipping on a soft drink, Jessica thought about her life. So many questions kept popping into her mind: *How will I be able to provide for my baby when I can barely take care of myself? Will I even know how to be a mother to a tiny newborn baby? Will my relationship with my boyfriend be different once a baby gets here?* So many unknowns . . . she had no idea what to expect, and just trying to picture it all consumed her thoughts.

God had been in those thoughts a lot lately, and she was beginning to think that maybe she really did need Him in her life. She was tired of feeling alone and empty. Pulling out her binder from a class she'd been attending at church, she began flipping through it. Each page was full of Scriptures and encouraging notes, and she landed on a page that said "Believe With Your Heart" at the top. She read through it, even the prayer at the end. She felt a stirring in her heart—and knew it was time. The leaders had talked throughout the semester about giving your whole heart to God, and Jessica felt like she was finally ready to surrender everything. Her way wasn't working; she knew that. She was ready to accept Jesus as her Lord and Savior and be made new.

She closed her eyes and whispered the prayer: *Dear heavenly Father, I realize I'm empty inside and that Your spirit is not in me. I have lived a life separated from You, and now I want to live in relationship with You. Thank You for forgiving my sinfulness and for paying for my sins through Jesus' death on the cross. I receive Your forgiveness. I surrender my will to You now, and ask You to take over my life and take up residence in my heart. Lord, make me new.*

Looking at her watch, she realized it was time to get back to work. She wiped her eyes, put her books back in her bag, and hurried to her usual post at the window. Once she had settled in, a young man drove up with a big smile. He said, "Hi. I'm not here to order food. I was just driving down the road and the Lord told me to turn around and tell the person at the drive-thru window that He loves you and not to worry about anything, that He was going to take care of you and to just trust Him."

With that, he drove away. Jessica was shocked. *Did that just happen?* Not five minutes after accepting Jesus into her heart and life, He found a way to say exactly what she needed to hear. Her faith in God had been renewed that day, and she knew that she and her baby were going to be just fine.

❧ *Brandi* ❧

 Sometimes there is an exception to a rule and a rule to any exception.

Brandi was twenty years old and just a few weeks away from her due date; she'd found out she was pregnant after she had been married for only eight months. They never really used birth control because her husband, Brody, believed that you didn't use protection once you were married.

She took a test on Christmas Eve, and it was positive. She poked Brody awake to tell him the news, he groggily asked if she was certain, and then rolled back over and fell back to sleep.

Christmas Day arrived with a schedule full of holiday festivities with his family. Brandi waited to see if Brody was ever going to mention it, but he never did—in fact, he wasn't talking to her at all. *Isn't this what he wanted? Why do I have this feeling like he is angry?*

On the ride home from the visit with family, Brody rode in the passenger seat as she drove. She noticed her cell phone vibrating with a text message alert. It was from Brody . . . but he was sitting right next to her? *I can't do this. I can't be a father. I want to have my own life.*

She immediately pulled over the car and yelled at him, "What are you saying? Why are you texting me when I'm sitting right next to you? Can we talk about this? Why would you not want this baby? We've always talked about having a family! What is wrong with you?" Brody kept his mouth closed and would not talk to her. Brandi could not understand why he was acting this way, but it was just the beginning.

Brody now slept in the living area, and would make comments like, "You know, Brandi, if you got an abortion, I would stay with you," or "You know what? You can't even take care of a dog, there is no way you could take care of a baby. You might as well kill it now because you're just going to end up killing it later."

A few weeks later, he was ready for her to leave. Brandi was crushed.

Brand-new newlyweds, not even married a year, only nineteen years old and already her husband is leaving her and wants a divorce . . . because she was pregnant. And she had nowhere to go, since for the past six months he had made certain she did not speak with her own family. Nor did he allow her to have friends; he wanted to control everything. No Facebook, no texting; he even would take her car keys during the day while he was at work so he knew she was at home. He didn't want her to have a job or any contact with the outside world besides his family on holidays.

The last day she lived with Brody, he came home from work and pulled something out of his jacket pocket and started twirling it around on his finger. It was a gun.

He kept twirling it around and said, "Are you going to have an abortion or not?"

She nervously replied, "No." Then, swallowing the lump in her throat, Brandi asked, "Is that for me?"

Brody replied, "I haven't quite figured out a way to get away with it."

She knew he meant it.

Her mother showed up a few hours later, only aware that her daughter was in some sort of trouble. Brandi had thrown together a bag of clothes and overnight essentials and left everything, even her car, since Brody had taken the keys with him when he left. On the car ride home, she broke down and told her mom everything that had been happening. When Brody's parents heard about everything that had happened, they urged Brody to at least give Brandi her car and allow her time to retrieve her other belongings.

When Brandi arrived with her parents, all her stuff had been thrown in boxes by the front door, even all of the pictures of them together. As she walked through to make sure that he had not forgotten anything, she noticed women's clothes in the closet, an extra tooth-brush on the sink, and small items everywhere she looked. It was evident another woman was already living there. She found out just a few months later that his new girlfriend, Lexi, was pregnant as well.

When Brandi first arrived at Embrace Grace, very near the end of her pregnancy, she had so much unfor-giveness and resentment toward her husband and even her child. But when she gave birth to Shane, her heart started softening. She started looking at the world a little differently. She loved her baby so much.

Brody wanted to sign over his parental rights, but his mother and his lawyer both advised not to in case he ever changed his mind later and wanted to see his son. Brandi was completely on her own and scared, but she knew God would take care of her and Shane, and that He obviously had a plan for both of them.

Toward the end of our semester at Embrace Grace,

we do a special night where we let go of any unforgive-
ness or resentment that we have carried in our hearts.
Brandi was finally ready to let it all go and move for-
ward, just her and her baby. She prayed a simple prayer,
*"God I want to let go of my fears and worries and hurt.
I want to lay them at Your feet. I want to let go of Brody
and Lexi and give them to You. I release them all to You!
I want to be set free! The chains will be bound and broken!
Thank You for letting me let it go!"*

Brandi developed a good relationship with Brody's
mother, even though Brody himself would have nothing
to do with her or Shane. Brody's mom loved Shane and
spent time with him every chance she got, so Brandi
couldn't wait to call her and tell her how God had
healed her heart when she prayed that simple prayer.

Brody's mom asked, "About what time did you pray
this prayer last night?" Brandi thought it was a weird
question, but answered, "About 9:30 p.m., why?"

Brody's mom started crying and said, "Well, you're
not going to believe this, but I was sitting at the kitchen
table last night with Lexi and at about 10:00, her eyes
got really big like she just had a major thought. Lexi
said, 'I have to fix things with Brandi. I haven't treated
her right. She is a lot stronger than I could ever be, and
I need to message her and apologize to her for all that
I've done.'"

Brandi couldn't believe what she was hearing; sure enough, at 10:10 p.m., Lexi had sent her an apology, and it sounded sincere. She had already let go of the hurt in her heart but just seeing the acknowledgment of wrongdoing from one of the people that had hurt her so much just seemed to bring complete closure in every way.

Most of Brandi's pregnancy doesn't hold the best memories for her; but once she allowed God into her heart, everything changed. There was hope. Her life wasn't over; a fresh start was just beginning. Just for her and Shane.

Brody has only seen Shane once, during a court hearing. Brandi has done it all on her own with God's help. She has always loved the name Shane, and shortly after giving birth, she realized that his name meant "God's Gift." Even through all the sadness and hurt, there was this amazing blessing growing inside of her; she didn't even realize it until she laid eyes on him. Even in the hard stuff, God gives us blessings.

Dianna

I remember the first time Dianna came to class. The girls took turns going around the room, sharing due dates and what their relationship was like with their "baby daddy." When we got to Dianna, the tears just started flowing before she could even speak. She just shook her head in silence, with tears pouring from her eyes. We knew we needed to move on, and hoped that God would do a work in her tender heart.

When Dianna was only fifteen months old, her family was hit with a devastating tragedy: her baby brother James had been born with digestive issues, and died shortly after birth. The sadness left their family broken; it was hard to know how to pick up the pieces and for her parents to emotionally and physically be there for everyone. To lose their child before he was old enough to speak his first word was so hard to grasp. Life moved on, but it felt like a piece of their hearts died with their son that day.

Growing up, Dianna had felt very close to her family and always knew she had them to rely on when she needed them, but things were slowly falling apart. Her parents were on the brink of divorce, and with so much heaviness and sadness at home, she was always trying to find things to do that would keep her busy. She needed an escape.

At age twelve, Dianna became very sick and missed a lot of school. Her stomach was constantly giving her trouble, and she was vomiting all the time; the doctor discovered a tumor in her stomach. Thankfully, the tumor was benign but due to missing so much school, Dianna began homeschooling.

That following year, Dianna began a relationship with a man she met on a social networking site. Her age on her profile was listed as much older than she really was, and she always looked older, so he never doubted she was lying about her age. The more they chatted online, the more her feelings for him developed. He was twenty years old. After hanging out together a couple times, Dianna lost her virginity. She was thirteen.

Soon after, her father was transferred from Chicago

to Texas. She settled into her new town, but continued to hang around with an older crowd. Her friends would offer her alcohol and drugs, and she would say yes so she wouldn't look immature to them. She would lie to her parents about her whereabouts and the company she was keeping.

At fifteen, she truly began to hate her life. She was already starting to feel addicted to alcohol, she was smoking weed and her appetite for both was never satisfied. The doctors had diagnosed her with bipolar disorder, but she never took her medicine. Deep down, she knew she was headed down the wrong path.

One day, she tried to end it all with a bottle of pills. Her mother, Julie, found her on the floor, unable to even stand. That was just the first of several more attempts at taking her own life.

Now sixteen, she still looked much older . . . or maybe it was that no one cared enough to question her age. And since she hung out with much older people, she could get into clubs without being checked for I.D.; but she had a fake one on hand, just in case.

Soon enough, Dianna was trying harder drugs. And deep down, she felt like she was always being taken advantage of . . . and sometimes, even by the people whom she trusted the most. At seventeen years old, she was raped by the older brother of her very best friend.

Dianna decided not to press charges since she was close to his family; she was concerned that it might cause a lot of drama—especially after confiding in his sister, her best friend, and she didn't believe her.

As much as she tried to blow the whole thing off, the rape left a hole inside her of pain that she could never figure out how to fix. She tried her hardest to block out the memories of that night the only way she knew how to: more drugs and alcohol.

A few months later, Dianna met a new guy at a hotel party. They were running errands together and they stopped in the grocery store parking lot, where he attempted to rape her. Dianna panicked, and begged him to just run in to the store first and to go get her a Red Bull and some cigarettes—anything to get him to stop. As soon as he was in the store and out of sight, she put the van in reverse and raced out of the parking lot.

When Dianna arrived home, she showed her mother the marks on her neck, arms, and legs. Julie was upset and immediately called the police; unfortunately, they could not help her or do anything, because it was her word against his.

She was so sick of the life she was living and people constantly taking advantage of her; but at this point, Dianna would have to hit rock bottom before she would finally find the courage to stop. And her rock bottom came soon enough.

Julie received a phone call from the hospital that a car registered in her name was found behind a local bar with three teenagers inside. The report was that two males and one female were unconscious and had been taken by ambulance to the local hospital. She raced to the hospital and spoke to the woman at the front desk.

The woman confirmed the report—but the female brought in to the hospital was not her daughter, it was a different girl who was a few years older.

Julie was confused, *Had Dianna been in the car too? Was she dead somewhere? Had she been taken?* She asked to see the girl to help her locate Dianna.

When she entered the room, Julie realized it *was* Dianna; her only identification had been her fake I.D., so the hospital had checked her in under the name on the license.

While Julie was relieved that Dianna was alive, she was also angry and disappointed. Dianna, along with her friends, were found passed out in the car with their hearts barely beating; their clothes had to be cut off. Their bodies were in so much shock that they had even urinated on themselves while unconscious.

That night Dianna realized the severity of the problem she had—yet for some reason, she still was alive.

What was her purpose in living? Why had God spared her time and time again when she had made such a mess of her life so far?

She was sick of partying and sick of the people she hung out with. She was sick of her thoughts and just tired of her life. She was ready for a change and a fresh start. So for the next few months, Dianna stayed busy to try to keep her past regrets from creeping in to her thoughts . . . *the different guys that had taken advantage of her . . . the night she almost died . . . all the other crazy days and nights she had survived . . .*

Dianna continued to stay clean and sober. She worked two jobs to keep from thinking about her past, one of which was in modeling. The pay wasn't great, but it was easy money. Through the agency, modeling jobs were slow to come in, so she would occasionally look online for others. Most of the sessions were for wedding dresses, and she always brought a friend so she wasn't alone. One day she saw an ad for modeling that paid well, but she couldn't find any friends to go with her. Since she needed the money, she went alone.

She found the location inviting and welcoming— fresh paint, white picket fence, and brightly colored flowers lining the walkway—no visible red flags. Yet Dianna began to feel uneasy. Something seemed off, though she couldn't explain it. But she really needed the money . . . and the ad seemed legitimate. Maybe she could just step in for a moment and if it seemed bad, she could just make a dash for the door.

A young man about mid-twenties had on jeans and a nice shirt. He smiled and asked her to come in. She stepped inside and noticed the apartment was very bare. There were no photos on the wall, only a couch with a television on a stand. It was just empty. There was no clothes rack, lights, or any other indications for a photo session. The man offered her a drink; she sipped as she tried to think of an escape route. He asked her to sit down on the couch, and she did what she was told—he was much bigger, and she knew she could not overpower him.

The next few moments were difficult to remember; it was as if time stood still. He climbed on top of her . . . he took her clothes off . . . Dianna can't explain why, but she just went into a state of shock.

God please, make this stop. I'm so tired of living my life this way. I need You to help me to make good decisions. I need You to save me. . . . Show me Your purpose for my life.

After he finished, he threw a wad of money at her. Dianna fled the apartment, leaving the money where it had landed.

Shame and guilt set in. She felt dirty, even though she never wanted that to happen. A few weeks later,

Dianna began getting sick. She threw up constantly, and it lasted longer than a typical stomach virus. Dianna finally drove herself to the doctor, who asked if she could be pregnant. Dianna quickly answered and told the doctor no, she'd had a birth control shot. At the doctor's suggestion, she took the test anyway.

When the results were positive, Dianna just couldn't believe it and insisted on another test. The second one had the same result. She cried as she told the doctor what could be the only way she had gotten pregnant . . . the man with the modeling job. She couldn't even say the R word. Her worst fear was coming true.

Everything about that night had been so hazy and foggy; she couldn't remember details, like his face. On the other hand, she was thankful she couldn't remember much, fearful of how she might feel if she could recall his face.

She considered abortion, but she never gave it much more thought than that. How could she rob an innocent person of a life—a person who had had nothing to do with this violent act?

Dianna started having panic attacks, and wondered if she should just give the baby up for adoption. Her mother felt so helpless; she wished she could take the pain away. Many nights Dianna would cry to her father, who remained supportive and would tell her, "This baby is part of our family. If you can't take care of it, then your mother and I will adopt her and she will be ours. Everything will be okay." Dianna had nightmares about the night of the rape; sometimes, her thoughts would get so dark and heavy she would think about taking her own life . . . but then she thought about the baby. No matter the circumstances, Dianna was determined to give this baby a chance at life.

Embrace Grace invited *Invisible Chains* author Kerrie Oles to share her story of how she broke the chains and patterns in her own life and give her testimony of how God was always with her. Kerrie encouraged all the girls in the class to write down their own personal "chains," all their past hurts and disappointments. That night, Dianna was finally able to say the word: *rape*. As the tears flowed, she forgave the man that had raped her, as well as finally forgiving herself for all the decisions she regretted in her past.

Her heart felt so much lighter that night as God started showing her how this baby was a gift, an answer to her prayers. This baby was the change that she had been asking for; this baby had saved her life.

Dianna's water broke on Christmas Eve. Every emotion she had bottled up inside began to flow as she held her daughter for the first time. When she looked at her baby, with her dark skin and long dark hair, she didn't see the man who raped her; she didn't see ugliness or darkness. She saw a beautiful life that God had given her, and she was perfect. Out of all the women in the world, He chose Dianna to be the mother of this baby girl, Ireland.

Dianna is now bold in sharing her story, and still feels a release from putting everything "out there." It's so amazing how God takes our ashes and makes something beautiful out of it. His promise is to turn everything to good for those that love Him, and He gave Dianna something good. She can't imagine her life without sweet baby Ireland.

Julie and Dianna now lead an Embrace Grace program at their own home church, and Dianna is a voice for the babies who have none. As a victim of rape and a crisis pregnancy, she loves to share how Ireland has a destiny and purpose for her life . . . and how God gave her a tiny baby who saved her own life.

❧ *Allison* ❧

The morning after the party, Allison checked her messages; the cute boy from the party had found her. She had seen him before at different parties, but had never spoken with him before. He had dark hair and bright blue eyes and a mysterious look about him that kept her attention. Her heart skipped a beat as she read the message. His name was Zach, and he was interested in hanging out. After a few light-hearted texts back and forth, she agreed to meet him.

They were together for the next few years; when Allison wasn't in school or working, she spent every available moment with Zach. They fell in love.

Attending cosmetology school, Allison's schedule became increasingly hectic as she left school to wait tables until late in the evening—all to pay for school and other bills. This left Zach to have what he called "*bro* nights" with his buddies, including his good friend, Jared. Allison got upset when Zach hung out with Jared due to his reputation of drug use and hanging out with the wrong crowd; she felt like Jared was a bad influence.

Zach was introduced to a drug by Jared called "Bars," a commonly prescribed medication used frequently on the streets because it gives a false sense of well-being. It has horrible side effects of severe depression and if taken in large amounts, causes you to black out and have no memory of what happened when you took them.

Bars would make Zach irate; Allison could barely understand the words coming out of his mouth, and it would take a long time to get him calmed down again. He would become so angry, he would call Allison or family members hurtful names and sometimes even punch walls. After these episodes ended, he would almost immediately fall asleep. When he finally awoke the next morning, he would have no memory of what had happened.

This began a vicious cycle of Allison and Zach breaking up and getting back together. Each time they reconciled, Zach would do well for several months at a time. They would plan their future and dream about possibly having a family someday, while enjoying ordinary activities together in the present. But eventually, Zach would slip up and do Bars again, and the cycle continued.

After a few years of dating, Allison started noticing that she felt very tired all the time. She would fall asleep if she sat still longer than just a couple of minutes. Her appetite increased, and she realized something was not right. So she took a pregnancy test.

When the results showed positive, Allison could not stop crying. She already knew she wanted to spend the rest of her life with Zach, but this was not the way she envisioned it happening. She had so many unknowns and questions about her future. *What about school and my job? What is my mother going to say? What is Zach's family going to say?*

Instead of telling Zach, she handed him the pregnancy test while the tears started flowing down her cheeks again. He looked at her and then back down at the test and then back up at her again, confused. He threw questions at her left and right, trying to figure out what she was thinking and feeling. Finally, Zach wrapped his arms around her and held her as his mind raced, silently asking the same questions Allison was worried about.

Life kept going with their busy schedules of work and school, and although they didn't talk much about the pregnancy, Zach remained patient and supportive. When she eventually told her mother and sister, they were shocked—but not angry. They sat down with her, gave her a hug, and told her that it would all work out.

A week later, after going out to dinner with Zach's family, Allison was in the kitchen putting stuff away and Zach was at the table eating his leftovers already. Zach's dad walked in the room and asked, "Allison, are you pregnant?" She stood motionless. *How did he know?*

Allison nodded her head slowly, surprised by his reaction—he smiled big, calling for his wife to come into the kitchen to hear the news. Zach comes from a big Italian family, and this baby would be the first grandbaby born into the family.

After all the reactions Allison envisioned, she never dreamed both sets of parents would respond with joy and support.

At their first appointment at their local pregnancy resource clinic, Allison and Zach watched a video showing them their different options on abortion, adoption, and keeping their baby. After Zach saw the gruesome dangers of what an abortion will do not only to the baby, but that the procedure was life-threatening to the mother, he knew that there was no way he would let Allison risk never being able to have a child in the future. Or even worse, lose her own life. Even though they hadn't planned on having a baby so soon, they knew they could make it work.

A few days later, Allison had dozed off; she vaguely remembered Zach trying to wake her up. They had just gotten into an argument earlier in the evening, Allison was so tired and just wanted to sleep. Instead, she woke up suddenly to water being poured all over her and Zach screaming incoherently again.

"I hope this baby dies! I don't want to be with you! I can't stand you. You try to control me and I can't take it anymore!" He just kept screaming at her. Her heart sank as she realized he had been out with Jared again and had done Bars. How could he do this when he had been doing so well? She thought he had meant it this time and that he would stay clean for his child and for her.

The next morning, Allison's mother came and picked her up. Allison was steadfast—she was finished with Zach. None of his begging or promises worked this time. She knew that if there was any hope at all for them to get married someday and be a happy family, he had to kick this drug habit first.

Over the next few weeks, Zach kept texting, but Allison did her best to ignore him. She was still angry and just tired of everything.

She did, however, elect to put her anger aside to include Zach in her next sonogram appointment—or at least, tried to. She texted and called many times, but he never responded.

When Zach finally returned Allison's call the following day, Allison answered with, "We're having a girl and her name is Audrina." Zach was quiet. He seemed to be processing what Allison was saying. He desperately wanted to be a family with Allison and straighten up his life once and for all. If she just gave him one more chance. . . . He asked if he could please go with her to her next sonogram appointment, and she agreed.

Over the course of the next few weeks, Zach used that time to show Allison how he had changed by taking her out on dates and telling her how everything was going to be different this time. He really wanted them to be a family. The day of the appointment, he begged Allison to take him back, asked her to marry him, and talked about how he couldn't wait to be a father to Audrina.

Allison's heart broke for him. As much as she wanted that, too, with him, she knew it was too soon to tell if he was sincere.

A few days later, on a beautiful Saturday afternoon, Zach called and as soon as Allison answered, she regretted having done so. He was screaming so loud she had to pull the phone away from her ear to even begin to understand what he was saying. Something

about his father being upset at everyone in the family
. . . even her. And why she still would not say *yes* and
just marry him.

Zach had done it again.

With tremendous strength, she said, "I'm not even
going to talk to you right now. My baby is more important than this. I don't need you." Then she hung up.
Allison knew what she needed—church. Actually, she
needed *God* to show her what to do, and how to go
forward and be strong for her baby . . . even if she had
to do it without Zach.

She was getting ready for church and glanced at her
phone; she had three missed calls from Zach's father,
which was unusual. She thought, *I am going to have a
good day today and I'm going to church. I'm not going
to get involved in your personal family fights. I'm staying
out of it and moving on.* Her phone rang—it was Zach's
father again—and Allison stared at her phone trying to
decide if she should answer it.

"Hello?"

Zach's father said, "Allison, I need to talk to your
mother." An odd request, but she complied, handing off
the phone to her mother. Allison watched her mother's
face go pale while listening; she clutched the back of the
dining room chair tighter as if to keep from falling over.

Zach had overdosed.

They quickly drove the few miles to Zach's house and before Allison's mother could even stop the car and put it in park, Allison jumped out and raced to the front door. There were family members everywhere—aunts, uncles, and cousins. Where is Zach? Was he at the hospital? Allison demanded to see him.

Everyone looked around at each other uncomfortably. Zach's mother could barely get the words out. "Baby, he's gone. He's no longer with us. The paramedics said he was already gone when they arrived."

Allison couldn't believe it. *I just spoke with him yesterday! There is no way he is really dead.* She started crying, but still felt like her heart was still not fully grasping everything.

In the days before the funeral, she felt like a zombie. She would check her phone, thinking he was about to call or text. Zach was only twenty-one. He was about to be a father. How can this be? Why did it have to end like this? He didn't want to do drugs anymore.

Information started leaking out that Jared had introduced him to heroin the night he died. He was still high on the Bars, then did heroin on top of it. His heart couldn't keep up. His heart had simply stopped beating.

Allison didn't want to go to the funeral but she knew she had to; she slid their baby girl's sonogram picture into his hand and laid a letter she wrote to him on his chest. She just wanted one last hug. She wanted one last kiss. She needed one last memory with him. As they closed the door on the casket, she felt her knees buckle underneath her. He was gone. Forever.

The days following the funeral felt so foggy and hazy. Allison and Zach had done everything together, and now she was doing everything alone. She wrestled with a lot of "what-ifs": *What if she had taken him back when he begged her to? What if she had spoken to him on the phone a little longer and listened to why he was upset that last time they spoke? What if she had given him another chance?*

Allison sank into a deep depression. She went to the doctor to have him check the baby and make sure Audrina was still healthy and strong. Allison had a hard time eating, so they needed to get her on a medication to help with that. Her mom brought her to church to get help—which is how Allison found Embrace Grace.

A few months after Zach's passing, Allison gave birth to Audrina. She came out looking just like her father. Allison wasn't sure how that was going to make her feel; every thought of him still brought up sadness because he wasn't here with her to enjoy that moment. But Allison bonded and grew closer to Audrina, who gave her a new outlook on life.

Today, Allison often thinks about if she had never gotten pregnant with Audrina, where would she be? She is so thankful for her gift of life, even during a season of death. Audrina gave Allison a bright future.

Sadie

Expecting the unexpected is hard to do.

Especially when I was unexpectedly expecting you.

At just six weeks I saw you first, I thought, although unexpected, it could be much worse.

Then at twenty weeks I saw you again, tiny toes and fingers, expectedly all ten!

Later I saw you at week thirty-five, much bigger as expected and made me feel so alive!

Last but not least, week forty came along, I met my sweet Judah, meaning praise, my sweet song.

I now know to expect the unexpected is always for the best because God gave me you, the ultimate present, better than all the rest.

Written by Sadie, nineteen years old and pregnant with an unexpected blessing.

Brittany

I hated being the oldest child. And growing up in a military family was definitely not a "walk in the park."

When I was eight, I learned that the man I knew as my daddy wasn't my biological father at all; it began when my younger sister and I were walking home from school, and one of our friends started teasing me because we barely looked related. This didn't sit well in the back of my mind, and I couldn't stop thinking about it. When we got home from school, I questioned my parents and they dropped the bombshell on me—"Daddy" had adopted me. And my world shattered.

Who was my real father? My parents wouldn't tell me anything until I was much older . . . but by then, he had passed away. So I never knew him. I decided if

I ever had a child, I would make sure I stayed with the father—no matter what.

By age twenty, I was well into the drug party scene, working as a stripper to pay for my habit, on top of being in several toxic relationships. I was smoking, drinking, partying, and having sex. Everything your parents tell you not to do, I was doing—anything to fill this emptiness that only God can fill, though I just couldn't see it at the time.

I had been in a roller-coaster relationship with a guy for a while that ended with him cheating on me, and getting the other girl pregnant. When he and his new girlfriend had a huge fight several months later, he called me. Things happened . . . and the cycle continued.

I began to sink into a horrible depression. I found myself regretting almost everything I had ever done over the past few years. I was so ashamed; I had no hope, and I only saw one way out. One night I fell to my knees and looked up and said, *"God, if You are real . . . and if there is any room for love for me, give me one good reason to keep on living because I can't do this anymore."*

Silence. *He doesn't even hear me. He doesn't see me.* There was my answer. I decided I would give God twenty-four hours to do something to prove He's real. I had already made my plan of how I would be ending my life the very next night.

The next morning, my sister came into the bathroom and handed me something. "Brit, you've been really moody, and your boobs are, like, three sizes bigger. Take this and let me know." I looked down to see that she had given me a pregnancy test. I rolled my eyes.

After the longest five minutes ever, there it was in very small digital print: *pregnant.*

It was a lot to process. While I had always dreamed of being a mother someday, I had my fair share of tears. Over the course of the pregnancy, I got more and more excited about this life I had inside of me. I wanted to love and nurture this child. I wanted to make up for the mistakes I had made in my life. I realized that God had given me my reason to live. I asked Him to give me a reason, and He answered my prayer.

I finally gave birth to a beautiful baby girl that I named Keira Sage, which means little/dark peace/wisdom.

My daughter saved my life.

This unexpected miracle that God blessed me with gave me a reason to live—but it took a while before I accepted Jesus into my heart. I went through Embrace Grace and they planted seeds in my heart; anytime I was quiet and alone with my baby, I would go back to Scriptures that I remembered . . . that God had a plan and purpose for my life, a plan for me to prosper and He has a good future for me and gives me hope (Jer. 29:11). I wanted to wait until the right time and make sure I was ready to surrender my life.

That day came in the form of a crossroad.

I had a big decision to make about my future. I wasn't sure if I should stay in the city where I had been living, or move back home so Keira and I could have a fresh start, just the two of us. I asked God to show me what to do. I drove to work, knowing I had to make my decision soon.

My shift began and a customer came up to me out of the blue, asking if he could share something with me. He said, "God wants you to know that the light is there. Whatever you are struggling with is almost over and you can do this. Be patient and you can make it through. Just accept Him into your life."

He sees me! He knows me! Overwhelmed with that thought, that night I prayed and asked Jesus to come into my heart. I was ready, and knew that God had always been with me, and now I knew that He heard me. I moved back home because I felt like that was where God was leading me. I ended up meeting an amazing man who loved Keira and me. I'm now a newlywed! No one ever expected me to get married, let alone be a good mother.

God has a reason for everything, and everything

I've gone through has helped me become the woman, mother, and wife God intended me to me.

I raised Keira alone until she was nine months old, but God gave me the strength to keep going forward every day. I even came to know Jesus through this. I couldn't deny anymore that there is a God and He sees me. He knows me and He loves me.

ᘓ𓆸 *Sarah* 𓆸ᘔ

Sarah was nineteen, pregnant by a guy she never really knew and didn't even really like very much. She was in a band and often drank, smoked pot, and stayed out late; she struggled with an eating disorder; and basically, Sarah was very unhappy.

One day, she told us the story about when she first found out she was pregnant.

Sarah had begun to suspect something was off, so she bought a pregnancy test and took it in her dad's bathroom. She couldn't believe it when she read the word *pregnant* on that little white stick. Maybe it was defective? Her heart sank as a huge mix of crazy thoughts and emotions swirled inside of her.

She knew that abortion was her only option. There was no thinking about it—she could never raise a child, she was too young. She had never even changed a diaper! She had no idea how to be a parent! But she also had no idea how she was going to manage scraping the money together to have the abortion.

Her mind raced constantly. *How could this have happened? I slept with a guy I just met and then got pregnant? Who does that? What kind of person am I? I don't want to be pregnant and I don't want a baby!* She even thought of starving herself until she was sure the fetus was dead.

Struggling with morning sickness and nausea, she began to realize that it is nearly impossible to *not* eat when you're pregnant. She felt she had to go back to her original plan—abortion. She spent weeks searching online for information on the procedure and any kind of financial assistance that might be available. The more time she spent thinking, searching, and stressing, the more real the pregnancy felt. Her heart sank a little further as each day passed; she needed to make a decision quickly.

First, she tried to explain herself to the baby. One night she said to us:

> I knew I might see her in heaven one day, and I didn't want her to think that I was being self-ish (which really I was) or that I disliked her. I needed some time by myself to get control of my

thoughts. I went to a horrible Mexican restaurant and took with me a pen, paper, and enough money to buy queso dip (that baby always wanted cheese). I sat down to write and stared at the paper blankly for fifteen minutes, just trying to keep my composure and not cry.

I had so many confusing emotions. I kept thinking, *I have to do this. Anyone in my situation wouldn't have the baby either. There is no other way. I have way too many things going on in my life and plus, I would be a terrible mother. I will lose everything in my life if I have this baby. The baby will be better off not being born to someone like me who can't even love a person. I can't love anyone. Look at the things I've done.*

I took a deep breath and grabbed my pen. As I was holding it, those thoughts still echoed in my head: *baby . . . the baby, the baby, the baby,* over and over again. I couldn't think of *it* as a *baby,* or I would never be able to get rid of it and get my life back. I started writing . . .

Dear baby, I want you to know why I have to do this. I can't give you the love or the life that you need. I'm not ready to be a mom. I know you'll go to heaven because you're innocent and you'll be very happy there. Love . . .

I was stuck. I didn't know how to sign it.

After I began to sign the letter with the word *love* at the end, I just froze. I couldn't sign it "*Love*, Mom." It hurt too much even thinking the word *Mom* knowing what I was about to do. I finally just quickly signed it *Me*. I folded it up and put it in my pocket.

I did this all to try to make myself feel better but somehow, I left feeling much worse. When I got home, I decided to write a letter to my mom. Surprisingly, this letter was a lot easier than the first. After I finished, I went and handed her the letter, and then went outside to smoke a cigarette while she read it. It simply said: *I'm getting an abortion. Help me or don't help me, but I'm doing it.*

When she came outside after reading it, she had big tears in her eyes, but she wasn't mad. She told me immediately she would *not* help me have an abortion. She told my father, and he didn't freak out either. I asked him if he still loved me and he said that he did. But he couldn't even look at me for three weeks.

Sarah's situation was even more complicated because just a few short days after she had found out she was pregnant, Matt (the "baby daddy") came by her house to say good-bye; he was moving away. She had never loved him, or even really liked him, for that matter. It was a one-night stand that ended up being one night that would change her life forever. Sarah had a decision to make: Should she tell him she was pregnant with his kid? Or should she just let him walk out of her life forever? She still wasn't quite sure what she was doing, so she let him walk away.

After weeks of thinking she needed to get an abortion but never actually going through with it, Sarah decided to keep her baby.

When word got out, most of her friends walked away, one by one. Some of them called her out of the blue, making it very clear that they did not want to hang out with her anymore. She could no longer keep up with their fast-paced lifestyle, so they just went on and didn't look back. Even her band kicked her out—via text message—when they realized a pregnant lead singer wouldn't really give them the image they were trying to portray. Sarah was crushed.

But there were some beautiful moments too.

During her pregnancy, Sarah and her mother bonded like never before. For once, neither of them was selfish or self-absorbed, and everything they did was all about the baby. They brainstormed baby names together, throwing names out to see what the other thought. Her mother even made her breakfast every morning. Sarah was so thankful to be able to lean on her. Sarah also began dating a guy who surprised her with ice cream every night. Never in her life had she felt so full and so free, all at the same time.

One day during one of our weekly classes, she started to cry (which was rare for her) as God began to reveal Himself to her. She had known for a long time that God had been giving her some tough love, and she knew He wanted her to stop the lifestyle she had been living. She knew God was saying, "No more of this. No more self-destruction."

Since Sarah had difficulty making friends or nurturing relationships with people, even though she wanted them, she asked God to send an angel into her life so she wouldn't be alone.

That particular day in our class, while processing where her life had been, and where her life was now going, she had the realization that this little girl she was carrying was the answer to those prayers. With eyes full of happy tears, she told us, "When I feel lonely, I just sing to her or just talk to her. Her little kicks and squirms feel like hugs and kisses. I can see that the world isn't this dark, unforgiving, harsh place that I thought it was—and I never want my daughter to view the world that way either. What I thought was a punishment turned out to be God's greatest gift to me and I was so undeserving. I used to cry and ask God, 'What did I do to deserve this?' Now I just wonder what did I do to deserve this . . . this beautiful gift of life."

Sarah's life changed forever the day her beautiful baby was born. Nothing anyone said even mattered anymore, because now her little girl was right there in her arms. It was *real*. Her baby, whom she named Fiona, was perfect.

Once she got home and settled in, her motherly instinct kicked in and she was comfortable being a mommy. Her life had changed drastically.

A few months after the baby was born, I spent some time mentoring Sarah and hanging out with her; I enjoyed her company a lot. She was like this unique treasure box and every time I spent time with her, I would uncover more and more precious jewels inside of her.

One day she shared with me, "My life switched upside-down like crazy after my baby was born. It didn't totally happen at all at once, though. It took a while for me to realize that my daughter was going to need all of me . . . she made me want to be a better person. God lit a little fire under me and her name is Fiona.

"Since the day she was born, I've still made dumb mistakes. I always will, since I'm human. But God's presence in her is so clear to me. I still see with those new eyes He gave me in her. Every day a little bit more of her individuality is expressed and every day she brightens my life more and more. She reminds me to pray. She tells me, 'Don't give up, Mama. It's okay. Try again. You can do it!' Every decision I make now is made based on wanting a better life for the two of us.

"From the time we are young and able to think, we have big dreams of changing the world, becoming something, impacting someone's life, or just doing something everyone will see as extraordinary. A child doesn't change that; doesn't slow the momentum. Your child is the change the world needs; your child is what makes you something. You'll impact his/her life beyond measure, and becoming a mother is the most extraordinary thing you can do here on earth."

✿ *Jenn* ✿

Jenn was six years old when she was diagnosed.

Crohn's disease is an ongoing condition that causes inflammation of the digestive tract. When this disease is active, it causes intense pain as well as ulcers in the mouth and even more severe ulcers in the gut. So while all her friends would be out having the normal childhood adventures without a care in the world, Jenn would be at home in bed, doubled over in pain. There was no cure . . . only a prayer that she would go into remission.

Crohn's was not Jenn's only struggle; when she was only eight years old, a friend's father molested her, leaving scars on her heart that she could never quite shake. After many court battles and legal trials, her perpetrator never really got the justice he deserved—he only got probation. She never felt like she had any vindication. In addition, her verbally abusive father left her lacking the love and affirmation needed; Jenn was hungry for kind words, love, touch, and attention. As Jenn entered her teenage years, her heart hardened a bit; with as many obstacles and hurts she had already experienced, she concluded that God did not exist—otherwise, those things would have never happened to her.

At age fifteen, Jenn met a cute boy but felt a little guarded, having never dated before. One day they were hanging out at her friend's house when he asked if she wanted to see the shed. She agreed, not thinking anything of it. When she refused his advances, he forcibly took what he wanted, leaving her devastated.

When Jenn met Cole, she discovered different things that could temporarily numb the pain of her past. Cole always seemed to be partying, drinking, or doing drugs. He never complimented her, and wasn't even really nice to her but would every once in a while mention how maybe someday they would have a family together and live a good life. She wanted so badly to escape her reality, even if it meant making a commitment to someone like him. She desperately craved change but did not see any way out of the vicious cycle she found herself in . . . until she found out she was pregnant.

She couldn't believe it. She took two tests just to

be sure. Cole had talked about getting married at various times in their relationship, so she just knew that he would step up and make her his wife—right?

Instead, Cole just shut down. When she finally got him to open up to talk about it, his first words were, "It's a blob, not a baby." Jenn was devastated.

She was only a sophomore in high school, and had no one to talk to. When she had her first ultrasound, she saw for the first time the tiny arms and legs and the silhouette of a little baby on the screen—her heart melted. There was a living baby inside of her womb! Even though she was scared about her future and how everything was going to work out, a new spark of excitement and hope ignited inside of her and she was already feeling a love for this child she was carrying.

Showing the photos to Cole, she asked him how they made him feel. He answered, "Tired."

"They said it is probably a boy!"

"Oh." No connection. No emotion. No interest in being a father. Nothing.

She began to cry. Finally, Cole couldn't hold in his feelings anymore. "Consider your options, Jenn!"

That was the moment she realized her new reality: she was going to be a single mom.

She broke up with Cole immediately, but deep down held out hope that maybe after she left, he would realize what he had in her and want his family back together again. That moment never came; in fact, it gave him new freedom to party even more, without having to answer to anyone else.

At eighteen weeks, Jenn finally went to her first obstetrician appointment and spoke to the doctor about her medical history. Since there were a lot of potential complications that were beyond the scope of her OB/GYN's expertise, he required her to go and visit her Crohn's specialist and let them know that she was pregnant.

When she arrived at the specialist, Jenn thought about her life. Even though she still didn't know how she was going to do it all, she was pretty proud of herself for staying focused on the baby and trying to not let depression take over. She did have moments of tears, but she wouldn't let them last too long. She was just taking it one day at a time. She hoped for the best, and for a good report from the specialist.

The doctor came in holding the test results in her hand. She quietly closed the door and turned and looked Jenn in the eyes.

"You need to get an abortion. Your body can't handle being pregnant; carrying and delivering this baby could kill you, or the baby. I can't see you as a patient, you're too risky."

Jenn was shocked. She knew having Crohn's

complicated pregnancy, but she didn't know she would get this reaction from her doctor. She stared at the doctor, stunned. Because Jenn's case was severe, the doctor explained, best-case scenario would be a preterm baby with very low birth weight. She wouldn't be able to push a baby out because of the complications of the disease. If she was to go into labor and the doctors could not stop it, the effects could be devastating. If she made it, she would have to have a C-section. According to the doctor, abortion was the best option.

Jenn left the office with tears spilling down her cheeks. *How could this doctor—this woman—say these things to me? How does she expect me to kill my baby boy? He has a name! He has fingers and toes!*

A second doctor gave the same opinion as the first. Jenn became discouraged and desperate. She still didn't believe in God, but found herself praying: *God, if You're real, please let my baby be okay. Please let my baby be healthy and strong and not come too early. Please give me a sign that You are real. I promise to carry this baby—just please let him live!*

Eventually, she did find a Crohn's specialist willing to work with her OB/GYN. Were her prayers being answered?

In the midst of all this, Jenn stumbled upon a company that customized necklaces. She had one engraved with *I will carry you* as a promise to her baby. Throughout the pregnancy, even when things seemed scary, it was a reminder of her promise; it also reminded her to keep praying.

One day, Jenn was on Facebook and saw a status about something called "Embrace Grace." Jenn was still skeptical about trying out a church group; she still wasn't sure she believed in God. Lately, though, she had felt so drawn to this idea that someone created her, and that she had a purpose. Did God have something to do with it? That night, the speaker of the class talked about asking God for signs that He speaks to us. We just have to open our hearts and listen to His words.

Jenn closed her eyes and rested her head on her desk for a moment. She silently asked God to give her a sign. *God, if You're real, can You give me a sign? Will You speak to me?*

The leader's voice interrupted her thoughts. She had been following a blog about a woman who carried her baby even though the doctors thought there might not be very much hope that the baby was going to survive outside the womb. This woman had made a promise to carry her baby—and she had even had a custom necklace made.

It said, *I will carry you.*

Jenn couldn't believe what she was hearing. *How did*

she know? Did she see my necklace? That would be impossible—it was under her sweater. Her heart jumped and her eyes filled with tears. She had to know.

Quietly, she raised her hand in the back of the room. The leader called on her and Jenn asked, "Um, excuse me, can you tell me, did the baby live? I just need to know . . ."

The leader smiled and said, "Why yes, this baby did live. They have photographs capturing the moment they heard the baby's first cry, music to their ears. It was a beautiful moment. The baby is a few months old now, and doing well."

Jenn let the tears fall. At that moment, she knew God was going to take care of her baby.

A few months later, after very careful monitoring by her medical team, Jenn made it full term and delivered a healthy baby boy via C-section. It bears mentioning that the baby weighed a whopping nine pounds! The doctors couldn't believe it.

Now with God by her side, she felt like she could do anything. All the hard work was all for this moment. She was a mom, and all that mattered was her baby. She never knew she could love someone so much. And she hadn't known that Someone could love her so much. She knew both now.

❧ Tasha ❧

At only ten days old, too little to even realize or remember, Tasha's life drastically changed forever. Her mother dressed her newborn baby in her sleeper, tucked Tasha into her crib for the night, placed a baby bottle full of chocolate milk next to her in case she got hungry, packed up all her stuff in the car, and left . . . forever.

Tasha's father, Joe, worked the night shift and got a phone call in the middle of the night from one of his neighbors in his apartment complex. They thought it was odd that they saw Tasha's mom leaving with her car full of clothes and belongings, but without baby Tasha. Joe left his shift at work and raced home to find his house unlocked with the lights off. Thankfully, baby Tasha was still sound asleep in her crib. Joe had no idea how to raise a baby girl by himself, but he was determined to try.

Tasha's mother had a drug problem. At one point during her pregnancy, she had tried to sell Tasha for drug money. Joe knew that, but he still couldn't believe she would give their newborn chocolate milk, leave the door unlocked, not leave a note or anything, and just leave . . . but he knew deep down, that she really was not coming back.

Growing up, Tasha knew her family was different, but her father was a good man; still, there were those times when Tasha tried to ask "girly" questions like when she started her period for the first time or started liking boys. He seemed to freeze up and not know what to say; many times, Tasha was left to figure out that stuff on her own.

When Tasha turned thirteen, she couldn't quit thinking about her mother. *Why did she leave me as just a tiny baby? Where did she go? What has she been doing the past thirteen years? Couldn't she have called me at least to check on me?* She begged her father to please try to find her. She just wanted to spend a little time with her and get to know this woman that had given birth to her— and then walked out of her life. Joe finally agreed to try.

Joe went through the courts to track down his ex-wife. He was afraid for his daughter of what they might find. She might not even want to be found; would that hurt Tasha more? Or maybe his ex had changed, and things were different. Maybe she had tried to find them but she couldn't.

Joe tracked her down within a few months. He contacted her and told her that Tasha really wanted to see her. He couldn't tell whether she was glad or upset, but she finally agreed to see Tasha. They arranged their schedules so that Tasha's mom had her every other weekend, to try and develop a relationship with this daughter that she had walked out on thirteen years before.

When Tasha finally met her mother, she was glad to finally sit and just look at her, trying to piece together a puzzle that had had so many missing pieces for so long. On the other hand, however, she was disappointed to see a dark side of her mother—this, she wasn't prepared for. She seemed . . . off. When Tasha tried to ask a few questions, her mother would brush her aside by saying, "Don't go there."

During weekend visitation, Tasha just wanted to hang out with her mother and soak up every second with her, but it always seemed like she was annoyed. Her mother would do things that did not make sense, like talk or yell at the walls, or hole up in her room. She knew her mom had a history of drugs and alcohol, but couldn't decide if they'd had a permanent effect on her brain or if she was high; either way, Tasha was disappointed.

The new visitation plan only lasted a few months. One day, Tasha arrived at her mother's house at their regular meeting day and time, only to see the house was vacant. Everything was gone as if no one had ever lived there. *How could she have left so fast? I just saw her two weeks ago and now the house is empty?* Her mother's number had been disconnected, and Tasha had no other way to track her down.

This time, she was old enough for the impact of the abandonment to hurt her heart. *What is wrong with me? Why does my own mother continue to walk out of my life? How could she do this to me and not even let me know?*

A month after high school graduation, Tasha met a guy named Taylor. He didn't have a father growing up, so they felt connected. Their friendship quickly turned to a relationship, and they spent every chance they could together. After they had been dating just two months, Tasha started to realize that something was not right. She worked at a dog groomer's, and noticed that every time a new dog smell would hit her nose, she would race to the bathroom to throw up. Her breasts were sore and tender. She thought maybe it was from drinking too many sodas, and tried to push it all out of her mind.

A few weeks later, Joe had a doctor's appointment

scheduled for himself. Tasha asked if he could schedule one for her at the same time. She had not had a checkup in a while, and secretly she just knew something was not right. She needed to get to the bottom of whatever was going on.

When Tasha went in for her appointment, she finished explaining all her symptoms and the nurse asked, "When was the last time you had your period?"

Tasha's heart dropped; she knew enough from friends and health class that there was a reason the nurse was asking her this. *Could I really be pregnant? I think I'm a few weeks late . . . it's been a while since I had my period last. Oh God, please no. Don't let it be this. I just turned eighteen, I can't be.*

Tasha took the test and the nurse confirmed it. *How am I going to tell my dad I'm pregnant? This will crush him. I just graduated high school and now I'm pregnant? How can I take care of a baby? I have to pull myself together so Dad doesn't notice I've been crying. He'll worry about me.*

Tasha took a deep breath, quickly wiped her eyes, and faked a smile to meet her father. During the drive home she tried to think of the best time to tell him— and Taylor.

What is he going to say? He is even younger than me! His mother will be so upset. Will he leave me? Am I going to parent this baby alone? I'm going to be a mother . . . and I don't even know what a mother is! Will I bolt and run too? I'm so confused and I don't even know what to think.

After the initial shock, Taylor told her that he would be there for her and be a father to their baby—they could just figure it out together. His promises made Tasha feel a little better, knowing that she would not be walking this alone. But there was another hurdle to clear.

She took a deep breath and said, "Daddy, I need to talk to you."

As soon as the words came out, she just started crying and couldn't stop. Her dad sat up and knew something was very wrong.

"Honey, what is it? What's going on?"

Tasha tried to calm down. She took several breaths. "I don't know how to say this to you but when I went to the doctor the other day, I found out that, well, I'm pregnant."

Joe's jaw dropped and he was speechless.

Tasha continued by explaining that she understood this meant her life was taking a different turn than expected, but that she felt she could do this. She admitted that she didn't have all the answers, but was determined—she did know, however, that adoption and abortion were not options for her. She wanted the responsibility. Then she stopped, catching her breath. Joe looked at her for a long time.

Finally, he said, "I'm here for you, Tasha. I'll always be here. You know that. Is Taylor going to be there for you as well? Does he know?"

Tasha explained that Taylor was totally fine and that they were going to figure this out together. Joe got quiet again, and she knew he needed time to process the news. She left him alone with his thoughts.

Over the next few months, it seemed like things got back to normal for her friends and family. Life goes on, and they still had to work and keep going. Tasha, on the other hand, was on a mission to make sure she was completely prepared for this baby's arrival.

Always an organized, "checklist" kind of girl, Tasha made it her mission to find the baby items that she needed; part of being a good mother, she determined, started with being prepared. She knew she needed to get some items for the baby, and planning was key; neither she nor her father had much money, and Taylor's mother was helpful, but she knew that God would ultimately protect and provide for this baby.

It was finally time for Tasha to get her sonogram— she was very excited, and Taylor joined her. Looking at the screen, Taylor said, "I keep seeing two circles on the screen that pop up out of nowhere . . . does this baby have two heads?"

They were having twins—twin girls. What were they going to do? Tasha was finally to a point she was ready for one—but two? *How can I be a parent of two babies when I've never seen a mom parent even one?*

A few days later, Tasha and her father were in the waiting room of the food stamp office and she noticed a woman waiting with twin girls that looked to be toddler size. She tried to take mental notes of how the girls were interacting with each other and how the mother was talking to them; she was tempted to ask the mother some questions but just kept thinking that the woman would probably judge her because of her age. After a few minutes of watching them, Tasha excused herself to go to the bathroom.

When she returned, she noticed her dad talking to the woman. "Yes, my daughter is pregnant with twin girls and due in a few months. Oh, here she comes now!" Tasha felt her cheeks flush with embarrassment.

The woman looked at Tasha and said, "You look really young."

Tasha was prepared for that statement. "I know, I know. Trust me, I'm more shocked than you are."

The woman was quiet for a moment. Then she responded, "You know, I live really close to here and I have a lot of baby girl stuff we don't need any more: two car seats, two jumpers, two nursing pillows, two swings, a double stroller, and tons more. Do you want to swing by after your appointment and come get them all? You can have them."

Tasha was shocked. That was almost everything that they needed!

God really is taking care of the babies and me. He really does hear our prayers! He has this all planned out, even when I feel like I don't.

When she was thirty-five weeks, Tasha went in for a regular checkup. During the visit, they noticed her blood pressure was very high. When the nurse rechecked, it was still high, so they admitted Tasha into the hospital, where she remained on bed rest for a few weeks. Finally it was time!

As Tasha pushed out "Baby A," she could not stop the tears from flowing when she heard her baby cry for the first time. All the memories and time spent worrying about whether she would be a good mother or not seemed to get lost in the tears of her baby's cry. She had no doubt in her mind and heart at that moment, that she would be the best mother she could be—it wasn't even something she felt like she had to learn, it was something inside of her.

"Baby A" was named Lily.

Totally exhausted, Tasha just wanted to sleep, but the doctor announced it was time to start pushing again. She collected all the energy she had left for those final pushes that released "Baby B" into the world.

They named her Kristanna.

Tasha could hear both of her babies crying. She had never felt so much love and joy at one time. She knew that all she wanted was to nurture, love, and give to her babies for the rest of her life.

Tasha's whole life changed that day. Her faith continues to be strengthened by all the miracles God does in their life as she and Taylor continue to raise their sweet girls. He has never forgotten them. Tasha loves to start new traditions and create new legacies for her children to pass down to her children's children, doing things with her daughters that she never got to do with her own mother. Life is definitely hard sometimes, but she loves her girls more than anything in the world. She is thankful for the sweet double blessing that God gave her!

❧ Arielle ❧

For the longest time in my life, I made a vow that I would not become like the other women in my family . . . pregnant at a young age. I saw how hard it was for them, and I always thought I knew better.

For years, I denied to my mother that I was having sex. Finally, I told her I had lost my virginity a few months after my seventeenth birthday—but the truth was I had actually lost it at age fourteen. I wasn't a bad kid, or a troublemaker; I just felt unloved, unhappy, and alone. I grew up without a father in my life and at the time, I had just lost my four-year-old brother. I didn't know how to turn *to* God with all my pain and hurt; instead, I turned to everything *but* God.

When I left for college, I was so excited to have more freedom and fun. I wanted to concentrate on my future and plan for success. During the spring semester of my freshman year, I hung out with a guy I considered a close friend. We would smoke, drink, and just chill every chance we got. I knew he had a crush on me, but I had a boyfriend so our relationship remained strictly a friendship. After hanging out with him on the weekends, I would head back to school and continue my education on Monday mornings.

After Spring Break, I realized that I hadn't had a period in a while. I was due to start at the beginning of the month, but nothing ever happened. I wondered if I had gotten my dates mixed up, or maybe it was just stress that was making me so late. I was worried; this had never happened before.

My boyfriend and I decided to go to the free clinic right near my school so I could take a pregnancy test. The clinic confirmed my fear: I was pregnant. The volunteer tried to explain that I was about six weeks along, but I just kept thinking, *How could I be pregnant when I haven't had sex in a really long time? These dates have to be off. This doesn't make sense.*

I called my buddy to tell him the news. I couldn't believe what he said next: "Is it mine?"

I was shocked and confused. I said, "What do you

mean, is it yours? We have never had sex—EVER. How could it possibly be yours?"

He then dropped the bombshell.

He told me that a few weeks before, we were hanging out and I was high and drunk. I supposedly told him to take my clothes off and asked him to have sex. But I still don't remember this ever happening. *How could I have been so high that I blacked out and don't remember one thing from that night, but I was still able to tell him to take my clothes off? It doesn't make sense. And even if that were true, couldn't he have seen that I was not in the right state of mind to know what I was doing or saying and that he should keep his hands off of me? And if I was so convincing and asked him to do this, why didn't he use a condom?*

I was furious and outraged. The fact was, he took advantage of me when I was vulnerable. And now, I was in the same situation that I vowed I would never be in; I was another single and pregnant statistic in the world. I was so ashamed that I had let this happen to myself.

After weeks of praying and asking advice, I decided that I couldn't ever go through with an abortion. I was going to keep this baby. I had no idea what I was doing, but I felt in my heart that it was the right thing to do.

When I finally told my mother, she was upset; and I was not welcome back at home. So here I was, finishing up my spring semester of college, pregnant and homeless.

I moved in with someone I had known for only a few months, but she generously offered her apartment to me. I was four months pregnant, and my bump was just starting to show. Once I got all moved in and settled, I realized we had a major problem . . . she was behind on her rent, and we were facing eviction within a couple of weeks.

I had nowhere else to go; I was homeless, jobless, scared, and depressed. Desperate, I started researching shelters for young pregnant women and found an emergency program called Bridges Safe House. I called them, and they said they had a place for me when I was ready. The day finally came when our landlords locked the doors and we were officially kicked out.

I lived at Bridges for almost two weeks, and the staff was really sweet and helpful. During my time there, I had no usage of any of my technology. No phones, no television, and no computer. I had chores to do every day, classes to take, and videos to watch to prepare me for my life with my child. All I had were my belongings, books, and the one thing that became my best friend during that time—the Bible!

My ultrasound revealed I was having a baby girl, and I knew immediately that her name was Serenity Anaiah.

Serenity means *peacefulness*, and that is exactly what I felt. Yes, I was still homeless, but the more I spent time with God, the more He gave me a peace about my future. Even when everything was chaos around me, I had serenity.

I was only allowed to stay at Bridges a maximum of four weeks, so I needed God to show me where I was to go next.

I came across this amazing ministry called Mercy House. At the time, they did not have a physical house yet (they do now), so through their program, I could live with a "shepherding family"; the family would take me in and "adopt" me for the remainder of my pregnancy, and for a few weeks after Serenity was born. When I finally met my new family, I fell in love instantly. I had lots of love, attention, hope, and joy! I was given free chiropractic services, free midwife services, free counseling, help with my phone bill, and more. I met lots of nice new people and got involved in a lot of fun activities that were always to help prepare for my future. My shepherding family also served as foster parents, so I even got to work with children of all ages, from newborn to seven years old. I spoke at events and even got involved with Embrace Grace through the program.

It still amazed me that I was training myself to seek God for answers when I lived my own way for so long.

He was leading me to the perfect places, and I was so thankful for the way He had been taking care of me. I never had to sleep on the street. He always had a temporary home lined up for me, even when I couldn't see it.

God even restored my relationship with my mother. I finally had the courage to tell her the truth about how I got pregnant and for the first time, I felt no shame. I knew God had forgiven me, and she did too. I didn't have to hide my story anymore.

Finally, it was time for Serenity's arrival. I had waited so long to see her sweet face! The Mercy House program connected me with a birthing center that allowed me to welcome my baby into the world by giving birth in water. I did it all naturally, and true to her name, Serenity entered our world peacefully.

It's true, I may have become another statistic of being a young single mother, but I wouldn't have had it any other way. My child has changed my life for the better and I love being her mommy. I graduated from Mercy House shortly after the birth, and my mom welcomed me back home.

Recently, I moved to my hometown of St. Louis, Missouri. I am a hardworking mother with my own car and my own apartment. I give God all the credit for where I am now. All I had to do was just trust Him, listen to Him, and obey His words. I went from being homeless to now being a stable and working mom. I'm single again, but I'm not discouraged. My daughter is the most important person in my life and I am truly blessed to be able to be her momma. I went from being extremely depressed, alone and hopeless, blaming everything on not having a father in my life, to now being a truly happy and joyous person; the only Father I need is my heavenly Father.

Even when I didn't have a plan for my life, God had one for me all along, even before He formed me in my mother's womb. I am living out my destiny and until He brings me to my next season, I will enjoy and cherish being a mommy to my sweet baby Serenity.

Ashley

Ashley was ready for a fresh start—again. She had tried to start over so many times but somehow she always got sucked back into her old lifestyle.

This time, she knew things had to be different; because this time, she was pregnant.

Growing up in a Christian home, Ashley attended a private school. Her mother was always there for her, but her father was mostly absent. He paid his child support in a timely manner, but emotionally, he was very distant.

When Ashley was thirteen, her family moved about an hour away, where Ashley began attending public school. She tried her best to fit in. She needed friends, and one in particular captured her interest; his name was Dillon.

The relationship started the way most teenage relationships start—flirting, but sometimes being playfully mean to each other. He was always doing something to pester her, and their game went on for a while until they finally made a commitment to date only each other. They stayed together throughout high school, even when Dillon started hanging around the kids who smoked weed and were always getting drunk. Ashley really liked Dillon a lot, so his habits soon became her habits. Very quickly, Ashley became consumed in a life of heavy drinking, taking ecstasy, smoking all the time, and wearing clothes that she hoped would keep Dillon's attention.

By this time, Dillon was in and out of jail on a regular basis, sometimes for months at a time. Ashley would write him letters and visit every chance she got—she loved him so much. Ashley even finished high school early, so she could spend even more time with Dillon when he was finally released, and they could go right back to their bad habits.

Even though Ashley and her mother were no longer close—and, in fact, barely crossed paths—her mother would say, "I always pray for you and I leave you in God's hands."

When Ashley was only eighteen years old, she became pregnant. Dillon was adamant that she have an abortion. She felt like she didn't have a choice, and she felt like a soul was being sucked out of her body that day. It was so painful, not only physically but emotionally as well. Her heart ached and a part of her was missing.

After the procedure, she was resting at home and in terrible pain. She called Dillon and asked if he would come help take care of her. She didn't want to be alone after what she had just been through. Every time she stood up, she felt like her legs were going to buckle and she would pass out.

His response: "I'm with my friends right now."

She was crushed. Every time he had been in jail, she was always there for him. He was the one who told her to get the abortion, and now he couldn't even take time away from his friends to help take care of her.

Shortly after, Dillon started hanging out with a new set of friends that were into a completely different lifestyle, something Ashley had never encountered before. She trusted Dillon when he said that it was nothing to worry about and no big deal.

But his new friends were pimps.

Not the kind of pimps you see on the television with their flashy suits, top hats, and canes . . . these were real pimps, with real prostitutes, and Dillon was fascinated with the money they were making. He told Ashley, "All you do now is work and get your check every two weeks. This girl gets that same amount of money in five minutes! If you want me to love you, you need to start doing that too."

Ashley was desperate for Dillon to love her and keep her, so she agreed to try it.

There are two different types of prostitutes: street prostitutes walk around outside and solicit sex; high-class prostitutes are managed online and make a lot of money. With the latter, there was less competition, but more work to do. They posted beautiful pictures of themselves online and waited for someone to make an offer. Sometimes the high-class girls traveled across the United States to meet certain clients who could afford the transaction.

Ashley would get off work at her regular job, dress up, and wait for a customer to make an offer to meet. She just wanted to make Dillon happy. *If this is what it's going to take, then I will do it.*

Ashley continued this lifestyle for a long time. Sex for her was not pleasurable; it was a job. She had sex with every kind of man: married, young, old, and in-between. She had to make sure she was really high to be able to tune out what was happening. She had to get through one more, and then another, and then another, until she was finally done for the day and could spend time with Dillon. After she turned a trick, she and Dillon would go out and spend all the money she had made, wasting the night away. It was an ugly cycle.

Her mother continued to pray for Ashley.

One day, Ashley got a job off an elite website and flew to Pennsylvania to meet a john. When Ashley landed, she had a voicemail from her mom. It said, "I don't know what it is you're doing, but in my heart, I know it's not right."

Ashley did not have time to call her mom back; as soon as she met with her client to discuss what they were about to do, someone kicked in the hotel door and arrested Ashley right there for prostitution. She was frantic. She was in another state all by herself thousands of miles from home.

What was her mother going to say?

Although she was devastated, her mother agreed to help find an attorney in Pennsylvania. After a long, drawn-out process, the judge finally dismissed the charges and gave her a ticket for disorderly conduct.

When Ashley got home, reality set in hard. She had no money and her pimp boyfriend had recently gotten into the habit of beating her up all the time if he didn't agree with what she was saying or doing.

One night, a man called Ashley's phone and Dillon was convinced that she was cheating on him. He flew into a rage and he destroyed her apartment, tearing off doors, punching holes in the wall, breaking dishes, screaming at the top of his lungs.

Ashley was beaten to a point she had to go to the hospital. She had hit rock bottom.

Her car was repossessed, and she lost her apartment, her dignity, and self-worth. When Ashley returned home to Texas, her mother took one look at her and said, "Baby, we have to get you to church."

Church? If my mom only had a clue. I'm so ashamed. How can a church let me even walk in there? God doesn't want me. He doesn't love me. I've done too much. I'm on drugs and I have a pimp boyfriend.

Ashley tried Gateway Church in Southlake, Texas, and immediately felt a peace that she had not felt in years. She felt like she was home. She did not feel judged or looked down upon. She felt like she was ready for a change . . . but Dillon was back in California. Ironically, Ashley missed him.

Dillon would call and make promises that, deep down, she knew he would not keep; but she wanted to believe that this time, he would love her. It was all she ever wanted. It was all she ever knew. She eventually dropped everything and flew back to California to be with him. She needed food and a place to stay, which meant she needed money, and she needed it quick; it didn't take long for Ashley to return to prostitution.

One day, Ashley was sitting in her room by herself, in-between johns. She looked in the mirror—she no longer recognized the girl staring back at her. *God, what happened to me? Where am I? WHO am I? Why am I here at this point in my life? Why doesn't Dillon love me even after all I have done for him? Am I ugly? Is there something wrong with me? I feel so empty inside.*

She drank from sun up to sun down to drown out all the sadness and loneliness. A few weeks later, Ashley lost her job because Dillon had beat her up so badly that her bosses thought she was turning away business. Her face was bruised and her eye was black. Her lip was busted, and her earrings had been ripped straight through her earlobes. She was fired.

Again, Ashley needed to make fast money to stay in her hotel; she decided to become the "other kind" of prostitute. As she began walking the streets with her friend, her pants became saturated with blood—almost gushing. She had no idea what was happening, but she knew something was wrong. Ashley got checked into the emergency room, where they ran tests and checked all that they could before the doctor came in with the results of the blood work. Finally, the doctor closed the door behind him and said, "So you're due in January of next year."

Ashley said, "Due for what?" She thought he meant

the medical bill that she had no idea how she was going to pay.

He responded, "You're nine weeks pregnant."

What? How? Why? I've been on birth contro. There is no way!

The doctor assured her that the baby was healthy and doing fine. He said that sometimes women that are pregnant and under stress can bleed out and the baby was just fine.

Ashley was paralyzed with fear. She had been through one abortion already, and there was no way she could go through that again. Her heart still hurt over losing that baby.

But God how can I be a mom? I have zero dollars to my name. I have no house, no car, and I can't provide for myself. I've been drinking and I'm on drugs. What am I going to do with a baby?

Even though she desperately didn't want to have an abortion, she started thinking that maybe she had no other choice.

There is no way I can have this baby. There has to be a way out of this! Maybe if I keep drinking, maybe this baby will stop growing and I will miscarry.

Eventually, Ashley couldn't keep that lifestyle up; her body didn't even crave the alcohol anymore. She was just so tired of everything. All she did was give all her money to Dillon while she was starving herself. She looked awful from the heavy partying. She couldn't manage it all anymore, so Ashley returned to Texas—but this time, she knew it was different.

She had a baby inside of her, and she was going to stay pregnant. Dillon started calling again with the same promises. Ashley knew Dillon was the father, because she had always used double protection with her johns; but she knew that being apart from him was the only way there could ever be a chance for her and her baby. He could not be an active part of her life, or their child's.

A family friend had told her mother about a class for single and pregnant girls. Ashley was not sure she wanted to try church again, now that she had fallen even more. She was ashamed to show up but her mom was not taking *no* for an answer.

Ashley loved the class immediately. She felt so comfortable and didn't feel like anyone was judging her. All the leaders had been in similar situations with their own pasts, and they were so encouraging. For once in her life, Ashley began to feel hope again. She was hungry to know God and that peace that comes from spending time with Him. She had never forgotten that feeling from when she was younger—but knew she had distanced herself from it.

Writing became Ashley's solace in this period of waiting and transition. She wasn't sure what her future held, so she just sat and wrote and let God speak to her through her writing. She loved going back through what she had written and seeing how God had started answering her prayers.

A few classes into the semester, we did our weekly "rose and thorn." Our "rose" was sharing the best thing that happened this week and our "thorn" was sharing the worst thing that happened. It was a great way for leaders to get a glimpse of what was happening in their worlds, and see how we could help.

That night, Ashley opened up and shared with us how her rose was that she really felt like God was clearly speaking to her more than ever, telling her that there was about to be a huge change in her life. While she and Dillon were not going to be together, she felt peace about it, because God told her that everything was going to be okay.

The very next week, Ashley came to class just a few minutes before it started and asked to speak to me privately. We went out into the hall and before she could even tell me, she just started crying so hard.

She finally forced the words out. "Amy, Dillon is dead. He's gone."

She couldn't go on any further. She just wept. I was speechless.

Apparently, Dillion had been at a party and four gunmen came up to his car and sprayed it with gunfire. A girlfriend of Ashley's had also been a casualty. Another friend who had witnessed the shooting called Ashley to let her know.

Ashley didn't know how or why she came to class the next night, but we all stopped what we were doing to pray for Ashley. As we laid hands on her, Ashley told me later that she was thinking, *Jesus, I know I'm here for a reason, but I need You to show me what for. I don't know what to do. I feel alone and I need You now more than ever. Please heal my broken heart. Please show me how to move forward from something like this.* After Ashley's silent prayer and while we were still praying, Ashley's baby kicked enough to make her jump. Right then and there, a peace washed over her and she felt an inexplicable change in her spirit.

Ashley knew once and for all that God had given her everything she needed to raise her baby. She knew she still had much healing to do, but that God's plans for her were purposeful.

Ashley delivered her healthy son a few months later, and said, "I always thought God would punish me for being a prostitute and a drug addict, and for lying to the people I loved the most. But instead, He made me a mom! What do you see when you see a mom? I see nothing but pure joy, happiness, a caretaker, a lover, a nurturer, a provider, a strong protector . . . and I was the complete opposite of all of those things, but He still made me a mom. I am now *all* of those things. He saved my life and gave me a gift. He gave me a destiny and purpose. He gave me a son to help me heal and grow. He gave me life so I could live."

❧ *Tiffany* ❧

Tiffany could not believe the two little lines showed up so fast: *Pregnant.*

She was in the restroom stall at Wal-Mart, of all places; her best friends were standing outside, waiting for the results as she just stood in silence staring at the stick.

At only fifteen years old, Tiffany had no idea how to even process this information; all she could do was walk outside with a fake smile on her face and say, "Well guys, I'm pregnant. I'm fine. Let's not let this ruin our day. Let's go do something. Everything is going to be okay."

Tiffany went through the motions of hanging out with friends, but inside, she was worried. *Dad is going to be so upset. Mom is going to freak out. I'm only fifteen.*

*And what about Chase? We broke up, and he is already
with someone else. How is he going to react when I tell him?*

She called Chase, her ex-boyfriend, to tell him the
news. His response was, "I'm not breaking up with my
girlfriend just because you're pregnant." That wasn't the
question on Tiffany's mind, as she had a lot more important things to be thinking about.

One day, she was in class when a voice came over
the intercom, paging her to the office. She thought it
was odd, but packed up her stuff and headed down.
The school nurse met her there and asked to speak to
her privately. "Tiffany, it has come to my attention that
you are pregnant. I just needed to let you know that I
have an obligation to call your parents within twenty-
four hours of being notified of pregnancies within the
school. So you can tell your parents tonight, or I can
call them tomorrow and let them know. When you get
home, call me if you want me to tell them for you. I'm
here for you and can help any way you need me to, or if
you have any questions at all."

Tiffany had put this off for as long as she could—she
didn't have a choice now.

Her day was interrupted again when her father came
to pick her up from school. *What is he doing here this
early? He never does this. Does he know something?*

She climbed into his truck, and he immediately

tossed an unopened box of pregnancy tests. She looked up at him, wondering what he knew.

"Your mom won't shut up," he said. "She thinks you're pregnant. I'm tired of hearing about it and I just want to get this over with. Can you just take a test and prove her wrong?"

How could Mom know? Then Tiffany remembered. A few weeks before, she had been jumping on the trampoline with her sisters and got sick several times. She had to ask everyone to stop jumping while she bent over the side to throw up. Tiffany had no idea at the time she was carrying a baby inside her womb.

As the pregnancy tests sat in her lap during the car ride home, she couldn't stop thinking about how this was playing out. *What am I going to do? How am I ever going to tell him? This is not happening!*

When Tiffany arrived back at the house, she took the box, went straight into the bathroom, and just started crying. She pulled out her cell phone and called the school nurse.

"I'm sitting in my bathtub right now and I don't want to tell my dad. Will you call him and tell him for me?" The nurse agreed. Tiffany sat in the tub for thirty minutes, clutching the unopened box of pregnancy tests. Tears flowed freely as she waited to hear her dad's reaction. Her phone rang.

"I told him and he's okay. He just wants you to come out and talk to him. Don't be scared. Everything is going to be okay."

Tiffany nervously came out to where her father was waiting to assure her that he was there for her and supportive of whatever decision she made.

Her mother, on the other hand, was upset and angry, and wanted her to get an abortion. Tiffany did not feel right about doing that and quickly rejected that option.

The three of them arranged a meeting to discuss how to move forward with the news. When they all sat down, Tiffany knew immediately that her mother must have been talking to her father, because both of her parents started explaining how abortion might be the best option for her. It was her sophomore year of high school, and she was about to make the varsity softball team.

"Just think about it," her mom said. "You can play softball again and move on with your life. You can just skip a few days of school and we'll tell everyone that you're not feeling well. All this will be put behind us and we can all just move on."

Tiffany was surprised that both of her parents were suggesting this. Finally, she agreed. She would have an abortion.

At the clinic, she lay back on the table while they

started a sonogram. They had the screen turned away from her while they glided the transducer over her belly. The nurse confirmed her pregnancy, told her she was about twelve weeks along, and then asked if Tiffany would like to see the sonogram; Tiffany nodded her head yes.

Tears began to flow as she saw this tiny baby. She could see a silhouette of a baby face with tiny arms and legs.

Pulling her shirt down, Tiffany ran out of the room and into the waiting area. She pulled her father outside and then just started crying. She didn't say a word as she handed him a printout of the sonogram.

Her dad looked down at the picture of his future grandchild and started crying. "I didn't really want to do this either. I'm sorry. I was a little scared about it and felt unsettled about you having an abortion, but I just thought for a moment it was the best solution—but it's really not. Let's go home. Everything is going to be okay. We'll get through this."

Over the next few months, Tiffany tried to picture what it would be like to have a baby and be a mother at her age. One day, as she and her dad were shopping for Christmas lights, her dad casually mentioned the idea of adoption. "They let you choose whether you want open or closed," he explained, "and how involved you want to be with your baby. It might be something to consider too."

Tiffany had heard of people doing this, but she didn't realize you could choose an open adoption. Maybe she could still be a part of her baby's life! *I'm just a sophomore in high school. I know we could find a way to get by . . . but I want more for this baby. I don't want it to just get by; I want it to have everything. God, please show me and make it clear this is the right choice.*

At the advice of her grandmother, Tiffany promised to look at some profiles of adoptive families to see if she could feel a heart connection with any of them. Tiffany received information on three different families, but one immediately stood out; there was just something about them that drew her in.

When Tiffany finally met Amber and Todd for the first time, she instantly felt that heart connection her grandma had mentioned. They made her feel so comfortable, and were so easy to talk to. They brought her a scrapbook that detailed their life so far; it contained photographs of their extended family members, their home, and all the trips they had taken. With every page turn of this precious book, Tiffany felt more and more settled on this amazing family. They shared with her their reasons for wanting to adopt.

Four years before, Amber had given birth to a baby

girl; ten months later, they lost her tragically to liver failure. While going through the loss and the ongoing healing of losing their child, they felt in their heart that they wanted another child, but had been unable to conceive.

Amber and Todd answered all of Tiffany's questions; they loved the idea of an open adoption, so Tiffany would be able to see her son when she could. They lived one state over, but not too far for a visit or a hug.

Tiffany left the meeting with a peace in her heart, but felt like she needed to pray more, just to make sure she was doing what God wanted her to do. For the next few weeks, she prayed every chance she got. Every time she prayed, that same peace would come over her when she thought about Amber and Todd as parents. She actually felt like she was having this baby so Amber and Todd could raise him or her. They had prayed for so long for a baby . . . and she was so happy that she was able to help their dream for a child come true. She knew this was God's plan. Even Chase had met them, and thought they were a perfect fit.

Two weeks after their meeting, Tiffany telephoned Amber and Todd to let them know her decision. "I feel a peace that you and Todd will be amazing parents for him," she explained to Amber, "and provide for him in every way that I couldn't."

Amber immediately started crying with joy—they had felt a connection with Tiffany too. "We've prayed for so long for this to happen!" she cried, expressing her gratitude over and over again.

Throughout the remainder of the pregnancy, Amber and Todd had active roles in preparing for their son's arrival, and became a source of encouragement for Tiffany. They made every effort to reassure her, talking through any worries, concerns, or fears she may have. They wanted to make sure that she had every question answered so that she felt complete peace on the day baby Roman would be born.

And that day finally arrived. Tiffany labored for hours with no progress, so the doctor decided to do a C-section. Per hospital policy, in an emergency C-section, only one person would be permitted in the room with her. Amber was a labor and delivery nurse, and Tiffany knew she could make her feel comfortable. She also wanted her to be able to be there when her son took his first breath of life and to hear his first cry out to the world. Amber was thrilled.

It was time! Amber had her camera ready and talked Tiffany through each step to help her not feel nervous. They held hands, anxiously waiting on the birth of this boy that they both loved so much. And a few moments later they heard it—the cry!

Amber and Tiffany immediately started crying; they could not contain the joy they felt in that moment. They had waited so long to see him and to hold him. The nurses wrapped him up and laid him next to Tiffany's face. She caressed his cheek as she admired how beautiful he was.

The nurses then began to care for Roman while the doctor was working on sewing Tiffany back up. Amber looked at Tiffany with tears in her eyes and mouthed the words, *Thank you.*

When Amber walked out to introduce baby Roman to everyone else, she just started crying so hard she could not even say a word. She was overwhelmed with joy, and this miracle she was holding in her arms; her prayers had been answered.

Tiffany signed all the pre-paperwork for the adoption and had scheduled to sign the official documents the day after release; she knew it was going to be hard to say good-bye. Tiffany couldn't stop the emotion from overflowing as she ran to her father and put her arms around him. He was crying too, as he held his daughter and looked over her shoulder at his grandson.

She then turned to hug Amber. Amber said, "Four years of hurt and pain, and thousands of dollars spent on making a day like this happen for us. And you just made it happen. Our prayers have been answered."

Todd placed his son in his car seat and everyone gathered around, including their nurse, and laid hands on the baby as Todd led in a sweet prayer.

"God, thank You so much for this amazing gift You've given all of us, this sweet baby boy. I know that You have created this child with an amazing destiny planned out for him. You thought of him before he was ever conceived and we know Your plans are great. Thank You for colliding all four of our lives from two different states together—we thank You so much for giving Tiffany the strength to sacrifice her body for nine months to not only save Roman's life but to give him an awesome future. We want Roman to grow up and know that every single person in this room loves him and cares for him so much. Help us steward Roman's gifts and be the best parents we can be to this priceless gift You've let us help raise and help him grow to be a godly man. We know that Roman's life will touch so many lives and be a living example of Your goodness and grace. Amen."

The next day, Tiffany arrived to sign over the parental rights of Roman. Amber and Todd sat her and Chase down, to just make sure they were okay with what they were doing. Tiffany still had overwhelming peace; she knew she was doing the right thing. She had no doubts or worries. She knew this was God's plan and she was happy and content. She felt God in the room as she signed the papers. She was giving her son an amazing life.

Tiffany always gets asked a lot of questions about her choice for adoption, like if she wished it had never happened, or if she could go back in time, whether she would do things differently. Her response is usually:

> I would never change anything. God has a plan for my life and I believe it was God's will for me to bless another family with my baby. Even now that my son is eighteen months old, I still have no regrets and such a peace about it. I love spending time with him, seeing him thrive and grow with his adoptive family who loves him so much. Going through this made me closer to God than I ever have been before, and it made me want to help other people. I appreciate life for everything it has to offer; even in the hard stuff, there is good stuff. When hard things come my way, my perspective is bigger. I look at it as a life lesson and try to choose good decisions for myself and the people involved. Roman has completely changed my life and made me a stronger person. I would do it all over again in a heartbeat.

❧ *Andrea* ❧

I was raised in a Christian home. Seriously—we never missed church, and I was extremely sheltered from the real world. But I knew early on that Jesus loved me, and I asked Him to come live in my heart when I was only five years old. My daddy even baptized me himself. When I was eight, we moved from the quiet country in East Texas to the busy city in Dallas. Having been so sheltered out in the country, I was unfamiliar with pop culture and, therefore, I was not very cool or popular.

My last year in middle school, I had a class with one of the popular girls in school that year. For some reason unknown to me, Katie took me under her wing. I didn't care why; I just knew she was going to be my ticket to popularity. Like magic, people started to notice me. Katie introduced me to new music, television shows, *boys*, skipping school, smoking, and drinking. I was really getting the hang of this popularity thing and didn't want to be remembered for my nerdy past; I chose to start high school across town where no one knew me. It was easy—just be bad, and you'll be cool.

My plan must have worked, because I was very popular in high school and was always getting into trouble. I thought I was invincible; I did whatever I wanted, whenever I wanted. I went to a lot of parties, experimented with drugs, skipped a lot of class, and was really obsessed with impressing guys. My friends and I would lie to our parents, telling them we were staying at each other's houses when, in fact, we would stay out all night—it sounds like a great plan to a teenager, but it sounds like a disaster waiting to happen if you are a parent.

On one of my many nights out, I found myself alone with an older guy; we were hooking up. I was so naive and didn't realize his intentions were for more than just a make-out session . . . I told him I didn't want to go any further once I realized what was happening. I'll never forget his response: *"Don't you think it's a little too late for that?"*

Scared and alone, I cowardly said nothing, and gave myself away to this complete stranger. I blamed myself in the end. After that, I found the phrase, "I have nothing left to lose" somehow comforting, and became promiscuous. I thought if I gave them what they wanted, they would love me. Regardless that I felt uncomfortable, I always felt like I was obligated to follow through; I would hear "his" voice in my head, saying, *"Don't you think it's a little too late for that?"*

My parents didn't even recognize me anymore. Eventually, I ended up in rehab—and I was only a sophomore in high school. I wasn't admitted for any specific drug; my parents simply stated that I was "out of control." Following rehab, I did well for a while (not that I had much of a choice), but things eventually went right back to the way they were.

Because I spent a lot of time *not* in class, I was getting nowhere in school. I had no plans for my future beyond doing what I wanted, when I wanted . . . and running wild.

I met Cameron when I started working at a local bar; he was friends with one of my coworkers, and happened to live down the street from me. He had his own house, which made it very convenient for me to do my partying and keep it hidden from my parents. I wasn't really interested in Cameron, just his house; but after a while I couldn't really tell the difference. Cameron had been through a lot of heartache in his life, and he was really trying to impress me.

We dated seriously, but it wasn't long before we started fighting all the time; I don't think you have ever met two people who are less compatible. During the years we spent on-again and off-again, I continued down this destructive path; I even ended up in jail for my sticky fingers.

With no serious direction for my life, and no real friends in my life, I tried for a new start and moved into a loft downtown with my brother. The owner at an adjacent bar, knowing I was underage, allowed me to work for him—and party with him and his staff. They all knew I lived next door, so they gave me no limit on drinks.

One day while at the loft, I went to the rooftop seeking something . . . I just didn't know what. Somehow, God led me to this verse, and I broke down:

> I waited patiently for the LORD, and He turned to me and heard my cry for help. He brought me up from a desolate pit, out of the muddy clay, and set my feet on a rock, making my steps secure. He put a new song in my mouth, a hymn of praise to our God. Many will see and fear and put their trust in the LORD. (Ps. 40:1–3)

I was in a slimy pit for sure, and needed someone to save me from it; I longed for my heart to sing a new song. But I didn't know what to do with these feelings at the time, so I continued on the only way I knew. Cameron would tell me I was drinking myself away, and that I was never going to find happiness that way. I kept asking God for a sign to show me what He wanted from me and what His plans were for me. A few weeks later, I realized I was late and took a pregnancy test—it came back positive.

We told my parents I was pregnant right away. Disappointed, they insisted that Cameron and I had to get married. I moved back in with my parents, and Cameron and I attended premarital counseling. Cameron gave me a promise ring, not an engagement ring; he was not ready to provide for a family.

We fought constantly, and we were actually advised by our counselor to split up. As much as making things work with my baby's father seemed like the best thing to do, I felt strongly that he was not God's plan for me; I returned the ring and broke up with Cameron.

I enrolled in a ten-week program to become a dental assistant. Around that time, a friend offered to throw me a baby shower. My father told me, "Unmarried women don't deserve to have baby showers, because baby showers are for celebrating married women for doing the right thing."

I knew in my heart that that couldn't be right; God had already forgiven me for my sin. *Isn't every life worthy of celebrating, no matter how it was conceived?* But this was God's first tug on my heart—He was asking me to submit.

> Everyone must submit to the governing authorities, for there is no authority except from God, and those that exist are instituted by God. So then, the one who resists the authority is opposing God's command, and those who oppose it will bring judgment on themselves. (Rom. 13:1–2)

For the first time in a long time, I decided to trust God instead of myself. I told my father I would respect his wishes and decline the offer.

My school, however, threw a little shower for me—and I even graduated with a job. What a blessing! No one expected me to get hired in my second trimester.

I was more alone in my pregnancy than I had been in years—no friends, no Cameron . . . my mother taught me that I could always talk to Jesus. Remembering this, I started praying hard. I found comfort in Scripture.

Dad invited me to a movie and concert at a church; the movie was called *Father of Lights*. During the event, I sat a few rows behind three girls who were holding hands and worshipping together. I was so jealous; I wanted to have that kind of friendship and sisterhood again, the kind you know would steer you toward Christ, and keep you accountable!

As I was walking out of my aisle to leave, I was stopped at the end of the row by one of the girls. Her name was Dylan, and she invited me to Embrace Grace—she wrote down her number and asked me to text her and let her know.

My Savior heard my cry. This church wanted to throw me a baby shower and celebrate this life inside of me. They saw *me*—not my sin! I had waited patiently, and He was definitely answering my prayers.

The first few sessions were full of life-changing stories from the leaders; this alone would have been enough to keep me going with my head up, but their love and support did not stop there. Things were falling into place—I had a job I loved, my parents' support, a plan for our future, the love and support of new friends in my life, and was seeking Christ in my daily life. But still I felt like I lacked peace with the father of the baby.

I just didn't want to hate him or feel animosity toward him. I wanted peace in my heart there too.

The next night was Embrace Grace. The leaders passed out little brown bags and told us to hold onto our presents until the end of class. Curiosity was getting to all of us, and finally, we got to open them. In there was a little piece of paper with a Scripture on it. Each person had a different one. Mine said: "Peace I leave with you. My peace I give to you. I do not give to you as the world gives. Your heart must not be troubled or fearful" (John 14:27).

There was my answer. God was telling me to give it up and let Him take control. He reminded me of Jeremiah 29:11: "'For I know the plans I have for you'— this is the LORD's declaration—'plans for your welfare, not for disaster, to give you a future and a hope.'" I repeated these two verses over and over and over in my head, meditating on them. If God is in control, then I cannot be. Miraculously, my heart began to ease at this realization, and I found peace.

I don't have to worry about tomorrow; I don't need to know what is going to happen next. He is going to take care of it. I don't know what tomorrow holds but I know God promises that He has an amazing plan for my future.

On October 17, my precious Bennett was born. I seemingly have done nothing right in my life to deserve this joy, but I was blessed with the gift of a child, regardless. A child who gave direction and purpose in my life that I could not find on my own. This is God's grace in my life . . . and this is not the end of our story. *It is only the beginning!*

Epilogue

A Bump in Life.

Speed bumps, potholes . . . they get in our way, slow us down, and sometimes point us in a different direction—one we haven't thought of yet. We take detours, think we're getting off track, but then begin to realize that although the new direction and destination may be different than the one we had planned, God hasn't gotten off track at all. He hasn't left us. Ever.

Getting to help girls in crisis pregnancies, I have been able to witness countless stories like the ones you have just read. As in these stories, God comes through for every girl who seeks Him—every single time. He never fails. He hasn't given up on you. He is just waiting for you to turn to Him.

In the story of the prodigal son, the father ran to his child, put a beautiful robe on his back and ring on his finger, and then celebrated with a big party that his child was finally home. That is what God is waiting to do with you. He wants to lavish you with His love and celebrate this child inside of you.

If you are experiencing an unplanned pregnancy, I want you to know that God *did* plan this life inside of you. He has a destiny and a purpose for this child, and it will be amazing. If things seem out of order and you can't see beyond the nine months of pregnancy, God sees. Every question that you might have about finances, a home, a job, childcare, the baby's father, your future husband—God already has the answer. Just trust Him and lean on Him during this season. Just take a deep breath, and take this one day at a time. The good news is, you don't have to have your life plan mapped out right now. Just trust God through this season. It may end up being the best season of your life—a season of miracles and blessings.

God never promised that we would have easy lives, but He did promise that He would always be there with you. He promised He would never leave you or abandon you. Some of His greatest revelations to us occur during times when we feel the most broken. He sees every tear that falls; His heart breaks with yours.

There is so much for you beyond what is going on right now. I know it's hard to see past this, but God promises to turn *all* things for good for those that love Him. He will turn this very situation for good. Open your heart to Him and invite Him in; listen to God's voice inside of you, and open your eyes to the signs He is giving you. He will show you that you and your baby are going to be fine. His will for your life is much greater than you could ever imagine or think.

So friend, it's time to brush yourself off, hold your head a little higher, and smile a little brighter because God wants to blow you away with His goodness and grace. Maybe you have an unplanned pregnancy right now, or you are a parent or loved one watching someone else go through it . . . or maybe you just are going through some challenges in your life right now. Whatever you are going through, God is there, waiting for you to run to Him. He will meet you where you are, and He will use this difficulty in your life to launch you into your destiny.

And those bumps? You'll begin to celebrate every one of them, as you walk forward into all He has for you. It's a bumpy—and beautiful—life!

Embrace Grace

Sometimes the hardest part is going through it alone.

Embrace Grace inspires and equips the church to love on single and pregnant girls. For more information or to find an Embrace Grace near you, go to www.iEmbrace Grace.com.

Author Information

Amy speaks frequently on the topic of Pro-Life. She can deliver a message of love and grace to inspire donors to help fund your ministry. If you are interested in finding out more, please visit her website at www.AmyFord.com.

You can also connect with Amy here:

Blog: www.iEmbraceGraceBlog.com

Twitter: twitter.com/amymford

Facebook: facebook.com/iembracegrace